THE BURNING FOREST

"I admire Simon Leys' clarity of style, a result of his disciplined and candid thinking. As he has a passion and respect for Chinese culture and the Chinese people, he cruelly debunks Western myths about contemporary China and we who are ignorant of its realities learn much from his terse presentation. His very tone is that of a man who is primarily concerned with truth."

—Czeslav Milosz

"Simon Leys' keen esthetic sense, his irreverence for political posturing and loathing of socialist cant have made him one of our most provocative and insightful critics of the Chinese Communist revolution. One may read him and weep, applaud, laugh or be outraged, but never bored."

—Orville Schell

"A brilliant, lively, amusing, clever, moving, and above all truth-telling book... it comes not a moment too soon."

—Irving Howe

"Finally, the book that demystifies China."

—Stanley Karnow

OTHER BOOKS BY SIMON LEYS

The Chairman's New Clothes
Chinese Shadows
Broken Images

AN OWL BOOK
A NEW REPUBLIC BOOK
HENRY HOLT AND COMPANY
NEW YORK

Simon Leys

The Burning Forest

ESSAYS ON CHINESE CULTURE AND POLITICS

Published by Henry Holt and Company, Inc., 521 Fifth Avenue,
New York, New York 10175.
Distributed in Canada by Fitzhenry & Whiteside Limited,
195 Allstate Parkway, Markham, Ontario L3R 4T8.

Originally published in France under the title *La forêt en feu*.

Library of Congress Cataloging-in-Publication Data
Leys, Simon, 1935–
The burning forest.
Translation of: La forêt en feu.
"An Owl book."
"A New Republic book."
Includes bibliographical references and index.
1. China—Civilization—Addresses, essays,
lectures. 2. China—Politics and government—
1949—Addresses, essays, lectures. I. Title.
DS721.L541613   1985   951   85-5521
ISBN 0-8050-0242-1 (hardbound)
ISBN 0-8050-0350-9 (paperback)

First published in hardcover by Henry Holt and Company, Inc.,
in January 1986.

First Owl Book Edition—1987.

Designer: Elissa Ichiyasu
Printed in the United States of America
10 9 8 7 6 5 4 3 2 1

Front cover illustration: *Forest Fire* by Luo Pin (1733–1799).
From an album on Jiang Kui's poems; ink and colors on paper.
Former Kawabata Collection, Japan.

ISBN 0-8050-0242-1 HARDBOUND
ISBN 0-8050-0350-9 PAPERBACK

The author is grateful to the following publications in which some of the chapters of this book appeared in a somewhat different or abridged form: *The Age Monthly Review,* "Fire Under the Ice: Lu Xun" (originally titled "Man of Ice and Fire," December 1981–January 1982); *Asian Studies Association of Australia Review,* "Orientalism and Sinology" (April 1984); *Le Débat,* "Peregrinations and Perplexities of Père Huc" (originally titled "Les tribulations d'un gascon en Chine: on les perplexités du Père Huc," July–August 1980); *Dissent,* "The Death of Lin Biao" (Summer 1983); *Encounter,* "The Double Vision of Han Suyin" (November 1980) and "The Fifth Modernization: Democracy" (November 1979); *The New Republic,* "Fools with Initiative" (March 10, 1979), "Peking Autumn" (originally titled "Chinese Despair," January 23, 1984), "Madness of the Wise: Ricci in China" (originally titled "The Church Goes to China," June 10, 1985); *Le Point,* "The Mosquito's Speech" (originally titled "Le discours du moustique," November 2, 1981); *Quadrant,* "Human Rights in China" (November 1978); *The Times Literary Supplement,* "The China Experts" (originally titled "All Change Among the China-watchers," March 6, 1981), "The Path of an Empty Boat: Zhou Enlai" (October 26, 1984).

All essays, except "Orientalism and Sinology," "Madness of the Wise: Ricci in China," "The Death of Lin Biao," "The Path of an Empty Boat: Zhou Enlai," and "Peking Autumn," were originally published in France under the title *La forêt en feu* by Hermann, éditeurs des sciences et des arts.

TO HAN-FANG ■

CONTENTS

FOREWORD

*Z*hou Lianggong, a great seventeenth-century scholar, wrote this fable:
   A flock of wild doves had for a while made their home in a certain forest. Later on, as they were passing again through the same woods, the doves discovered that the forest was engulfed in flames. They rushed at once to a creek, dipped their wings in the water, and, flying over the fire, scattered a few drops on the burning forest. As they frantically repeated this exercise, God told them: "Your intention is excellent; yet I wonder if it can be of much practical use." "We realize this," the birds replied, "but we used to live in this forest, and seeing it being destroyed breaks our hearts."

This book is, in a way, a continuation of *Broken Images*. Unlike the former collection, however, this one includes some perspectives on the cultural values of classical China, in order to suggest what the forest could represent for those who had the privilege to enter it before it was devastated. My hope is that the reader may thus more easily understand the deeper reason for an activity that otherwise could appear as futile as it is stubborn.

NB: Transcription of all Chinese names is in pinyin, except for a few names that have already entered English usage (Taoism, Confucius, Peking, Kuomintang).

· Culture

POETRY AND PAINTING: ASPECTS OF CHINESE CLASSICAL ESTHETICS

INTRODUCTORY NOTE

C hasing bits of truth is like catching butterflies: pin them down and they die. "As soon as one has finished saying something, it is no longer true." This observation by Thomas Merton* could serve as a warning for the reader and should indicate the proper way of perusing this little essay.

In Chinese classical studies, it is necessary to specialize. It is also impossible.

* Quoted by Monica Furlong, *Merton: A Biography* (London: Collins, 1980), 266.

Specialization is necessary. The wealth, scope, and diversity of Chinese culture wildly exceed the assimilating capacities and intellectual resources of any individual—and more particularly, they should drive to despair the wretched Western sinologists who, unlike their Chinese colleagues, did not have the chance to start their training in early childhood and thus approach their discipline at least fifteen years late.

Specialization is impossible. China is an organic entity, in which every element can be understood only when put under the light of other elements; these other elements can be fairly remote from the one that is under consideration—sometimes they do not even present any apparent connection with it. If he is not guided by a global intuition, the specialist remains forever condemned to the fate of the blind men in the well-known Buddhist parable: as they wanted to figure out what an elephant actually looked like, they groped, one for the trunk, one for the foot, one for the tail, and respectively concluded that an elephant was a kind of snake, was a kind of pillar, was a kind of broom.

Conversely, the global intuition that alone can grasp the essential nature of the subject (we shall have much need for it here) is invariably accompanied by a shocking neglect—if not downright ignorance—of surface details. This problem should not worry us too much, if we remember Lie Zi's story about the connoisseur of horses*: Bole, famous horse expert employed by the Duke of Qin, was becoming too old to pursue his search for the super-horse (to identify a super-horse is a business that requires exceptional perception). He recommended that the duke employ the services of his friend and colleague, a peddler named Jiufang Gao. Some time later, Jiufang Gao returned from his first mission and told the duke that he had found the supreme horse: "It is a white mare, belonging to a certain farmer in Shaqiu." The duke

---

* *Lie Zi* (Peking: Wenxue guji kanxingshe, 1956), book 8, 10–11.

sent for the animal, which actually proved to be a black stallion. "Your friend does not seem to be too competent after all," said the duke to Bole, but the latter, hearing that Jiufang Gao had mistaken a black stallion for a white mare, exclaimed: "Fantastic! He is even better than I thought. His perception of the essentials has now reached such a depth that all outer appearances are completely obliterated!"

In the course of this inquiry, I may well become guilty of simplifications verging on distortion that could at times induce the reader to suspect that here too the color and the sex of the beast have been mistaken. . . . Anyway, I shall seek no further excuses; after all, what is an enterprise like this but an attempt to prolong or to echo, however clumsily, those moments of bliss that we sometimes experience in our encounters with poems and paintings? (Can artistic and literary criticism have any other justification?)

China is a world. Any tourist who just spent two weeks there will tell you that much. (Though, in this case, I wonder if it is not a misunderstanding, as I doubt that the People's Republic has actually succeeded in preserving the *universality* that defined Chinese culture for some three thousand years. Of course, it is obviously too early now to attempt an evaluation of thirty years of illiterates' rule. But this is another story.)

Still, when it is applied to traditional China, this old cliché— as is often the case with commonplace statements—covers a truth that runs much deeper than one usually suspects while uttering it.

More exactly, one should say that China is a certain worldview, a way of conceiving the relations between man and the universe—a recipe for cosmic order.

The key concept of Chinese civilization is *harmony*; whether it is a matter of organizing human affairs within society or of attuning individuals to universal rhythms, this same search for harmony equally motivates Confucian wisdom and Taoist mysticism. In this respect, both schools appear complementary rather than antagonistic, and their main difference pertains to their area of application—social, exterior, and official for the former; spiritual, interior, and popular for the latter.

The various currents of Chinese thought all spring from one common cosmological source. This cosmology (its system is schematically summarized in the most ancient, precious, and obscure of all Chinese canonical treatises, *The Book of Changes*) describes all phenomena as being in a ceaseless state of flux. Permanent creation itself results from the marriage of two forces that oppose and complement each other. These two forces—or poles—represent a diversification of "having." "Having," in turn, is a product of "nonhaving" (*wu*),* a concept that is constantly mistranslated as "nothingness," whereas it rather corresponds to what Western philosophy would call "being." The Chinese thinkers have wisely considered that "being" can only be grasped *negatively:* the Absolute that could be defined and named, that could *have* qualifications, properties, and characteristics, or that could lend itself to all the limitations of a positive description, obviously cannot be the true Absolute—it merely belongs to the realm of "having," with its ephemeral and kaleidoscopic flow of phenomena. The process that we just sketched here does not form a mechanical chain, nor is it the outcome of a causal sequence. It could be better described as an organic circle within which various stages can simultaneously

* It may be amusing to note in passing that the latest discoveries of modern physics seem to verify the oldest notions of Chinese cosmology. Discarding the theory according to which the universe was the product of an explosion, some scientists are now propounding the theory of an original "bubble"; according to these views, as a cosmologist from MIT put it, "it is very tempting to assume that the universe emerged from nothing. . . . Possibly the most far-reaching recent development . . . in cosmology is [the] realization . . . that the universe is a free lunch." (*Newsweek*, June 7, 1982, 83.)

coexist. In the earliest texts, "nonhaving" seems sometimes to precede "having," but in later commentaries their relations are described in the form of an exchange, a dialectical union of complementary opposites, giving birth to one another.* "Being" is the fecund substratum, the field where "having" germinates—or, to put it in other words, emptiness is the space where all phenomena are nurtured. Thus, "being" can only be grasped in its hollowness: it is only its absence that can be delineated—in the same fashion as an intaglio seal shows its pattern through a blank: it is the *absence* of matter that reveals the design. The notion that the Absolute can only be suggested through emptiness presents momentous implications for Chinese esthetics, as we shall see later.

It is by cultivating the arts that a gentleman can actually realize the universal harmony that Chinese wisdom ascribes as his vocation: the supreme mission of a civilized man is to grasp the unifying principle of things, to set the world in order, to put himself in step with the dynamic rhythm of Creation.

The arts are essentially poetry, painting, and calligraphy; music should also be included here (for the Chinese scholar, music means only the zither *qin*); however, my incompetence in the latter field shall unfortunately prevent me from making more than passing reference to it.

A gentleman practices the arts in order to realize his own humanity. For this very reason, unlike all crafts (sculpture, carving, architecture, music played on vulgar instruments, and so forth), no art could constitute a professional, specialized activity. One should naturally be competent in all matters pertaining to poetry, calligraphy, and painting inasmuch as one is a gentleman, and no one, *unless* he is a gentleman, can achieve this com-

* On this question, one should read the masterful essay by A. C. Graham, "Being in Western Philosophy Compared with *Shih/fei* and *Yu/wu*," *Asia Major*, VII, 1959, 79–112.

petence. By definition, such fundamental activities can only be pursued by nonprofessionals; when it comes to living, aren't we all amateurs?

PAINTING AND POETRY

One exemplary figure embodied the union of painting and poetry: Wang Wei (699–761). He was one of China's greatest poets, and as a painter he has been credited with the invention of a new style that was eventually to constitute what is conventionally described today as "Chinese painting"—monochrome ink landscape executed with a calligraphic brush.

Su Dongpo (1036–1101), himself a most versatile literary and artistic genius of no lesser stature, commented on this subject: "In every poem by Wang Wei there is a painting, and in every one of his paintings there is a poem." This observation was subsequently quoted so often that it became a cliché. We must attempt to rediscover its original meaning and restore its full impact.*

First, this famous statement can be taken as a factual description. Consider, for instance, the following verses:

River waves flow beyond the world
Mountain mass hangs in half-emptiness . . .

---

* The best study on this subject is still Qian Zhongshu's "Zhongguo shi yu Zhongguo hua" in *Kaiming shudian ershi zhou nian jinian wenji* (Shanghai: Kaiming Shudian 1947). I have briefly outlined Qian's theory in *Les Propos sur la peinture de Shitao* (Brussels: Institut belge des hautes études chinoises, 1970, 98–99 [new edition: *Les Propos sur la peinture du Moine Citrouille-amère*, Paris: Hermann, 1984]). A new version of Qian's essay can be found in *Jiu wen si pian* (Shanghai: Shanghai guji chubanshe 1979).

When we read these words, they immediately conjure a vision that countless paintings have made familiar to us: a river flows toward a destination that lies beyond the page, carrying away a lonely little boat or a couple of drifting ducks, whereas in the empty expanse of the silk, a few faint touches of ink hint that, somewhere above the invisible riverbank, a mountain must be hiding in the mist.

However pertinent such a visual association may appear, we should keep in mind that this type of pictorial parallel is based on an anachronism: what the Tang poem just suggested is in fact a Song painting, which came into existence only some three hundred years later! As for Wang Wei's own paintings, although no original survives, the kind of image that various indirect witnesses enable us to reconstruct seems oddly out of place with the type of vision suggested by his poems. In contrast with the fluid and subtle economy of the poems, most probably his pictorial style was still painstakingly detailed and not yet free from archaic linear stiffness.

Moreover, if it is not wrong to say that painting and poetry express two sides of the same inspiration, it should be observed that it was only in the Yuan period—six centuries after Wang Wei— that scholars began to inscribe poems on their paintings, or to trace paintings under their poems, with the same brush and under the same impulsion. Wang Wei, painter and poet, may provide a convenient symbol of the union of these two arts; yet, in fact, his historical activity has very little relevance for our topic: the real meaning of Su Dongpo's statement lies elsewhere—and it could be summarized in a double axiom, which we shall try to analyze: *The esthetic principles and expressive techniques of poetry have a pictorial character. The esthetic principles and expressive techniques of painting have a poetical character.*

Whereas any poem, by its very nature, is normally expressed in the form of a sequence unfolding *in time*, Chinese poetry at-

tempts, in a way, to fit words *in space*.* The spatial potential of
the Chinese poem can be grasped first on a superficial level, if
we simply consider the fact that the poem can, and should, be
calligraphed; in this calligraphic form it can be exhibited and
contemplated just like a painting. However, the spatial quality
of the poem is not merely an outcome of Chinese writing; it has
a much more essential origin, which is to be found in the very
structure of the language. This could be well illustrated, for instance, by the use and technique of the "parallel verses," which
constitute a basic device of Chinese poetry.

Parallel couplets not only form the central core of all "regular
poems" (*lü shi*), they are also constantly used in all other pro-
sodic forms and can even be produced as independent units.
Schematically they are comprised of two symmetrical verses; in
each verse, every word possesses the same morphological status
and performs the same grammatical function as its symmetric
word in the other verse; whereas, in meaning, they are either
similar or, better, antithetical—which fully achieves their mirror
effect. Hence, a full enjoyment of a perfect couplet supposes a
double reading—both vertical and horizontal. For instance, in
the classic example (taken from Du Fu [712–770]),

Cicadas' voices gather in the old monastery

Birds' shadows fly over the cold pond

morphological and syntactical correspondences are rigorously
observed between the two lines, so as to turn each verse into a

---

* This phenomenon was analyzed with great perception and subtlety by François
Cheng in his book, *Chinese Poetic Writing* (Bloomington: Indiana University Press,
1982)—an admirable work to which I shall never adequately acknowledge all my
debts. Later on in this essay, I also borrow freely from James J. Y. Liu, *The Art of
Chinese Poetry* (Chicago: University of Chicago Press, 1962).

perfect match for the other; moreover, the interplay of the parallelisms enables us not only to read the lines vertically, but also to read them *across*: in this way, the "cicadas' voices" echo the "birds' shadows," "cold" prolongs "old," and the "monastery" is reflected in the "pond." From the first line to the second there is no logical sequence nor rational progression; what we observe here is not the linear unfolding of a discursive exposé but the circular coiling up of two contrasting images—nonsuccessive, simultaneous, closely imbricated into one another. Unlike the discursive mode of expression that forges ahead and develops in time, the parallel mode suspends the time flow and winds upon itself. There is no anteriority or posteriority between the two images: they are both autonomous *and* tightly welded together, like the two sides of the same coin. In a formally perfect couplet, it should even be possible to read the second sentence before the first without affecting the meaning (this possibility is well illustrated by the habit, in Chinese interiors, of hanging parallel sentences on both sides of a painting or of any other central ornament): they do not develop a discourse—together they organize a space.

The use of parallel sentences is not the only means by which the Chinese poetic language is brought close to pictorial expression. In a more general and fundamental fashion, the entire poem can turn into a pure juxtaposition of images. It is precisely this aspect of the Chinese art of poetry which, at the beginning of the twentieth century, fascinated Western poets, Ezra Pound in particular, and was to exert a significant influence on modern English poetry.

Some sinologists who know much and understand little have laughed at Pound's translations from classical Chinese. It is true that Pound knew very little Chinese and his translations are full of absurd mistakes. And yet, the fact that several excellent Chinese scholars have come to his defense should make us ponder: Pound's transpositions may be philologically preposterous, but they often achieve a structure and rhythm that are much closer to the original Chinese than are most scholarly attempts.*

Pound had a mistaken idea of the Chinese language, but his mistake was remarkably stimulating and fecund, as it was based on one important and accurate intuition. Pound correctly observed that a Chinese poem is not articulated upon a continuous, discursive thread, but that it flashes a discontinuous series of images (not unlike the successive frames of a film). Where he went astray was in seeking to explain the imagist properties of the Chinese poetical language by the alleged pictographic nature of Chinese writing. Actually, as any beginner learns after a couple of lessons, most Chinese characters are not "tiny pictures"— *stricto sensu* pictographs represent barely one percent of the Chinese lexicon—and yet the strange thing is that Pound never shed this mistaken notion; it inspired some of his most bizarre and unfortunate interpretations.

Actually, the real reasons that explain the imagist character of Chinese poetry, the factors that enable Chinese poets to deliver directly a series of perceptions without having to pass through the channels of grammatically organized discourse, pertain to two specific features of classical Chinese: morphological fluidity (the same word can be a noun or a verb or an adjective, according to the context) and, more importantly, syntactic flexibility (rules governing word order are reduced to a bare minimum; sentences can be without a verb; verbs can be without a

* See Wai-lim Yip, *Ezra Pound's Cathay* (Princeton, N.J.: Princeton University Press, 1969), and more specially, the very important article by Y. K. Kao and T. L. Mei, "Syntax, Diction and Imagery in T'ang Poetry," *Harvard Journal of Asiatic Studies*, 31 (1971): 51–136. Like François Cheng (mentioned earlier), Y. K. Kao provides us with fundamental insights on the nature of Chinese poetry. Without such guides, I would never have ventured to write this little essay. On the merits of Pound's translations, see also some interesting examples in S. W. Durrant, "On Translating *Lun Yü*," *Chinese Literature: Essays, Articles, Reviews*, 3, no. 1 (January 1981): 109–19.

subject; particles and grammatical trappings are practically non-existent).

Without venturing into the quicksands of linguistics, let us merely look at one or two examples. Wen Tingyun (818–872?) describes travelers departing before dawn in two famous verses that, translated word for word, read like this:

Roosters-sounds; thatch-inn; moon.
Man-footprint; plank-bridge; frost.

This collection of discontinuous and simultaneous perceptions, this series of scattered brushstrokes, can be reconstructed and interpreted in discursive language. We could say: "As one can still see the setting moon hanging over the thatched roof of the country inn, one hears roosters crowing everywhere. The travelers must have already left: their footprints are marked in the frost on the planks of the bridge." The pictorial resources of classical Chinese free the poet from all such verbose detours and from the need to express logical connections; he does not explain, he does not narrate—he makes us see and feel directly. What he presents the reader with is not a statement but an actual experience.

The same phenomenon is also nicely illustrated by the much-admired beginning of a poem attributed to Ma Zhiyuan (end of the thirteenth century).

Dead ivy; old tree; dusk crows.
Little bridge; running creek; cottage.
Ancient path; west wind; lean horse . . .

(It should be observed, however, that the imagist approach is not the exclusive mode of Chinese poetry; discursive language also has a part to play; in fact, Chinese prosody is based upon a dialectical combination of these two modes, and this combination finds its most systematic and sophisticated expression in the form of the "regular poem," *lü shi*. Nevertheless, it is true to say that the imagist language constitutes the *major* mode of Chinese poetry.)*

■

We have just seen how Chinese poetry attempts to borrow channels that normally belong to pictorial expression. We shall now examine how painting adopts the status and methods of poetry.

At first contact, the physical outlook of a Chinese painting already betrays its literary nature. Western painting, crafted by artisans, has the heavy, stiff, massive, and dumb presence of a piece of furniture: it hangs forever on its wall, gathering dust and fly droppings, awaiting a new coat of varnish every fifty years. Chinese painting, on the contrary, is mounted in the form of a scroll—which, historically, is related to the family of books. It genuinely belongs to the realm of the written word, as various expressions show: "to paint a painting" (*hua hua*) is a rather vulgar way of talking; the literate prefer to say: "to write a painting" (*xie hua*). The tools the writer needs—paper, ink, and brush—are sufficient for a painter. The mounting of the painting—fragile, quivering at the faintest breeze—forbids permanent exhibition and only allows one to display the painting for the time of an active and conscious *reading*.

The highest type of pictorial style is called *xie yi*, which means the style that *writes* the *meaning* of things (instead of describing their appearances or shapes). The guiding principle for this form of painting is "to express the idea without the brush having to run

* On the combination of discursive and imagist modes in Chinese poetry, see the article by Kao and Mei (cited above) and also the beautiful book by Kang-i Sun Chang, *The Evolution of Chinese Tz'u Poetry from the late T'ang to the Northern Sung* (Princeton, N.J.: Princeton University Press, 1980).

its full course" (*yi da bi bu dao*). The ideal painting is achieved not on paper, but in the mind of the spectator; for the painter, the whole skill consists in selecting those minimal visual clues that will allow the painting to reach its full and invisible blossoming in the viewer's imagination. This point leads us into another theme: the active function of emptiness—the role played by "blanks" in painting, by silence in music, the poems that lie beyond words. We shall come back to this question later on.

Finally, in parallel with the observations made earlier, on the spatial dimension of the poetical language, we should also note the time dimension that is expressed in a supremely sophisticated form of Chinese painting, the horizontal scroll (*shoujuan* or *changjuan*). The horizontal scroll has a physical structure that is identical to that of an archaic book; it cannot be hung, it can only be viewed on a table, through a progressive "reading" process—one hand unrolling one side of the scroll as the other hand rolls up the other side (in this way the viewer can himself select an infinite number of compositions, depending on which segments of the scroll he chooses to isolate as he pursues this scanning process). The eye is being led along the scroll, following an imaginary journey. Pictorial composition unfolds *in time*, like a poem or a piece of music; it starts with an overture, develops in a succession of movements, now slow, now quick, provides restful intervals, builds up tensions, reaches a climax, concludes with a finale.

COMMUNION WITH THE WORLD

Painters and poets are associated with the cosmic creation. Artistic creation participates in the dynamism of the universe.

Through his artistic activity a gentleman becomes both imitator of, and collaborator with, the Creator.* Hence, the poet Li He (790–816) could say:

The poet's brush completes the universal creation:
It is not Heaven's achievement.

Painters and art theoreticians expressed a similar idea, using practically the same words. Zhang Yanyuan (810?–880?) wrote: "Painting brings the finishing touch to the work of the universal Creator." It should be noted that in the West many artists reached similar conclusions. For them, however, these were empirical or intuitive observations; unlike their Chinese counterparts, they did not have the possibility to link such reflections to a cosmological system. To borrow an example close to home, I quote A. D. Hope's definition of poetry:

I have very little faith, as a professional critic of literature, in most of the descriptions or definitions of poetry on which the various schools depend. "The imitation of Nature," "the overflow of powerful emotions," a "criticism of life"—well, yes and no: none of them seem to me a satisfactory basis of criticism.
As a poet, I find them exasperating. I know of no definition of the nature and function of poetry that satisfied me better than . . . the view of poetry as a celebration, the celebration of the world by the creation of something that adds to and completes the order of Nature."†

---

* The expression "Creator," with a capital *C*, is used here as a convenient shorthand for what would otherwise require a lengthy paraphrase: "The inner driving force that moves the entire process of cosmic creation." The notion of a personal God, exterior to His creation, is utterly foreign to Chinese cosmology. (Classical Chinese treatises do sometimes speak of the Creator in a personified way, but this is a mere literary device—similar to our metaphors the "smiles" of Spring, the "anger" of the ocean, and so on.) *Natura naturans* would probably be a more appropriate term, but since I am trying to express myself in English, I am reluctant to use it.

† A. D. Hope, *The Pack of Autolycus* (Canberra: Australian National University Press, 1978).

It would be extremely easy to translate this last sentence into Chinese; in China, poets, painters, and esthetes have never stopped making this same statement for the last fifteen hundred years!

In Chinese poetry, communion with the universe is expressed by various means. We should first mention the unique resources the Chinese language affords poets (we already have alluded to it): the blurry fluidity of syntax and morphology that allows a permanent confusion between subject and object and establishes a sort of porosity, or permeability, between the poet and the surrounding world. A classical example can be found in the first two verses of Meng Haoran's (689–740) "Spring Morning":

Spring-time sleep is not aware of dawn;
Singing birds are heard everywhere . . .

Who is the sleeper? His person is nowhere described or defined—is it I or he or she? The poem suggests a depth of slumber in which the conscious self drifts and dissolves amid confused perceptions of dawn; singing birds vaguely heard in this sleep become the objects of a perception without subject.

A similar effect can be found in one of Wang Wei's most often quoted poems; here, moreover, the world is being personified— the natural surroundings become an active partner. These verses are often rendered in a way that, without being flatly wrong, considerably weakens the flavor of the poem:

In the empty mountains, no one is seen;
Yet, voices are being heard . . .

Actually, the poem literally says:

Empty mountain sees no one,
Only hears voices . . .

Quite naturally, it is with a poet such as Li Bai, deeply imbued with Taoist mysticism, that this personification of all things, this dialogue with the universe acquires full intensity and exuberance. As the poet identifies himself with the thing he contemplates, the subject eventually vanishes, totally absorbed into the object: perfect communion is achieved. We see this in the short poem "On Contemplating Mount Jingting":

All birds have flown away high in the sky;
One lazy cloud drifts alone.
Without tiring, I look at Mount Jingting, Mount Jingting looks
    at me;
Finally, there remains only Mount Jingting.

(Li Bai is a poet who can associate with mountains and rivers; he converses with the sun and the stars, as you and I chat with our old friends; he drinks at the banquet of the planets, he rides on the tails of comets. For instance, if one night there is no one with whom to share his bottle of wine, he improvises at once a little party with three guests—himself, the moon, and his own shadow—and this lively drinking bout ends with an appointment for another gathering next spring, in the Milky Way. . . .)

For the painters, the identification of the subject with the object assumes an even greater importance: nothing should come between the painter and the thing he observes. Su Dongpo expressed this most eloquently, as he was praising the bamboos painted by his friend Wen Tong: if the latter could achieve natural perfection in his art, it was because he had no more need to look at bamboos when painting them, as *he himself had become a bamboo.*

In order better to appreciate all the implications of such an attitude, it might be useful, by contrast, to refer back for a moment, to our own familiar world. In Sartre's *Nausea*—a good example of Western consciousness pushed to its paroxysm—there are two objects whose sight provokes in Roquentin a feeling of existential absurdity so acute that it results in actual retching: a pebble polished by the sea, and an oddly twisted tree root. It is interesting to note that, for Chinese esthetes, it was precisely such types of objects that could actually induce *ecstasy*—in fact, they were sought by connoisseurs and collectors even more avidly than the masterpieces of artists.

In order to dominate the natural world, Western man cut himself off from it. His aggressive, heroic, and conquering attitude toward the environment can be seen, for instance, in the art of classical gardens (every civilization always reveals its vision of the world in its gardens). Look at Versailles, where we see nature being distorted, bound, raped, cut, and remolded to conform to a purely human design; geometric plans are forced upon it, in complete disregard of its original essence. In such a rigorously anthropocentric perspective, any natural form, any spontaneous pattern that is not manmade and whose enigmatic complexity owes nothing to the human mind appears immediately threatening. Its irreducible and perplexing autonomy limits and challenges man's empire.

The Chinese, on the contrary, renounced domination of nature to remain in a state of communion with it (today, of course, is another story: the West, having reached the end of the road, belatedly discovers ecology and makes frantic attempts to negotiate some form of reconciliation with the natural environment, whereas China adopts with uncritical enthusiasm some of the most disastrous of our earlier attitudes). In complete contrast with Roquentin, *Homo occidentalis extremus*, who vomits in front of a stone whose grain and shape would have provoked utter bliss in a Chinese connoisseur, one thinks at once of the exemplary gesture of Mi Fu (1051–1107), one of the most admirable and typical exponents of Chinese estheticism at its climax. Mi, having reached the seat of his new posting in the provincial administration, put on his court attire, but instead of first paying a courtesy call to the local prefect, he went to present his respects to a rock that was famous for its fantastic shape (even today, "Mi Fu Bowing to the Stone" remains a subject very popular with painters). Needless to say, this spectacular initiative proved costly for his official career. Yet, by this very gesture, he made it clear for generations to come that, beyond all social hierarchies and conventions, there exists another set of priorities that cannot suffer any compromise. The strangely shaped rock, whose forms had not been carved by human hands, presented in its profile and its patina a direct imprint of the cosmic Creator; for this reason, it also constituted a supreme model and criterion in any creative undertaking. Painters are the privileged interpreters who can decipher and translate the universal consciousness that is written on rocks and clouds, in the twists of branches and roots, in the veins of the wood, in the billowing of mists and waves.

Probably the best way to examine this theme of "communion with the universe" in Chinese art is still to study the central role played by the concept of qi in the esthetic theories.

Qi is sometimes translated as "spirit," which could be misleading, unless one remains aware that the Chinese have a materialistic notion of spirit and a spiritualistic notion of matter. Far from being antithetical, the two elements indissolubly permeate each other. A good example of this conception can be found, for instance, in the well-known "Hymn of the Righteous Qi," written in the thirteenth century by Wen Tianxiang (this piece appears in every anthology, and when Chinese schools were still dispensing a literary education, all schoolchildren could recite it by heart). After having conquered China, the Mongol invaders wished to secure the cooperation of Wen, who had been a prestigious minister under the last Song emperor; Wen rejected their offers and was thrown into jail; there, waiting to be executed, he composed his famous "Hymn." In the introduction he wrote for his poem, he described the conditions in his prison: for many weeks, he says, he was surrounded by all kinds of pestilential qi—dampness, cold, filth, hunger, disease—and yet he observed that, alone among the other captives, he continuously enjoyed excellent health. His explanation was very simple: he was inhabited by a qi of righteousness—his unwavering loyalty toward the defeated dynasty—which naturally enabled him to repel the influences of all the nefarious qi. Whereas a Western mind would wish to distinguish between different realms, for the Chinese classical mentality, one single concept of qi can simultaneously cover physiological realities and abstract principles, material elements and spiritual forces. In Wen Tianxiang's world, it is quite normal that the fire of patriotism should melt ice, and that morality should overcome illness. (Would it be irrelevant to note in this connection that modern developments of psychosomatic medicine seem to confirm to some extent these traditional conceptions? Chinese yoga—which is called "discipline of the qi" and which is essentially based on meditation and breathing techniques—is now being used with some measure of success to cure various illnesses, and more particularly to treat certain forms of cancer.)

The literal meaning of qi is "breath" or "energy" (etymologically, the written character designates the steam produced by rice being cooked). In a broader and deeper sense, it describes the vital impulse, the inner dynamism of cosmic creation. For an artist, the most important task is to collect this energy within the macrocosmos that surrounds him, and to inject it into the microcosmos of his own work. To the extent that he succeeds in animating his painting with this universal breath, his very endeavor echoes the endeavors of the cosmic Creator.

Painting is thus, in a literal sense, an activity of *creation* and not of *imitation*; this is precisely the reason why it possesses a unique prestige, a sacred character. This notion is important and deserves to be carefully examined. In the West, both classical antiquity and Renaissance culture considered that art possessed an essentially *illusionist* nature. Thus, for instance, according to the well-known Greek anecdote, the competition between Parrhasios and Zeuxis ended in a double deceit: the birds that wanted to peck the grapes, and the spectators who wished to lift up the veil, eventually met with a mere painted board. Many legendary anecdotes about Renaissance artists reflect a similar mentality. Thus, Michelangelo is described as angrily hitting his *Moses*, because the statue would not talk or move: the lifeless marble infuriated him all the more for being so intensely lifelike. But in China the earliest anecdotes about famous artists all suggest a diametrically opposite conception; while Western artists applied their ingenuity to deceive the perceptions of the spectator, presenting him with skillful fictions, for a Chinese painter, the measure of success was not determined by his ability to fake reality but by his capacity to *summon* reality. The supreme quality of a painting did not depend on its illusionist power but on its efficient power; ultimately, painting achieved an actual grasp over reality, exerting a kind of "operative" power. A horse from the imperial stables began to limp after Han Gan had painted its portrait; it was subsequently found that the artist had forgotten to paint one of its hooves. Or again, the emperor who had commissioned Wu Daozi to paint a waterfall on a wall of the palace, a little later asked the painter to erase his painting; at night the noise of the water prevented him from sleeping.

In an archaic stage, painting was thus invested with magic powers. When magic matures, it becomes religion; in a sense, one might say that painting—more specifically *landscape painting*—constitutes the visible manifestation and the highest incarnation of China's true religion, which is a quest for cosmic harmony, an attempt to achieve communion with the world. Eventually the function of painting was redefined in esthetic

terms; still, in order to appreciate fully all the implications of the
esthetic concepts, one must keep in mind the archaic notions
(well illustrated by the magic anecdotes) from which they are de-
rived. The relation between the painted landscape and the natural landscape is not based on imitation or representation;
painting is not a symbol of the world, but proof of its *actual presence*. As a painter and theoretician of the eleventh century neatly
summarized it, the purpose of painting is not to describe the *appearances* of reality, but to manifest its truth. The painted landscape should be invested with all the efficient powers of
mountains and rivers; and if this can be achieved, it is because
the creator of the painting operates in union with the universal
Creator; his performance follows the same principles and develops along the same rhythms. Artistic creation and cosmic creation are parallel; they differ only in scale, not in nature.

Here again, it is striking to see how Western artists often arrived at similar conclusions by purely intuitive and empirical
means. Flaubert, for instance: "What seems to me the highest
(and the most difficult) thing in Art, is not the ability to provoke
laughter, or tears, or to make people horny or angry, but *to act
like Nature does*."* Or again, Claudel: "Art imitates Nature not
in its effects as such, but in its causes, in its 'manner,' in its
process, which are nothing but a participation in and a derivation
of actual objects, of the Art of God Himself: *ars imitatur Naturam
in sua operatione*."† Picasso put it more concisely but no less ex-
plicitly: "The question is not to imitate nature, but to work like
it."‡

It is in the theories of qi and of its action that we can find the

---

* Quoted by Maurice Nadeau in his introduction to the new edition of *Madame Bovary* (Paris: Folio, 1981), 6.

† P. Claudel, *Journal* I (Paris: Pléiade, 1968): 473.

‡ F. Gilot, *Vivre avec Picasso* (Paris: Calmann-Levy, 1965), 69.

best descriptions of the relation between artistic creation and cosmic creation. These theories occupy a central position in Chinese esthetics. At first the concept of qi might easily appear rather esoteric and abstruse to Western readers; in fact, it must be emphasized that it is also a concrete, practical, and technical notion that can be effectively demonstrated and experienced. Thus, for instance, successful transmission and expression of qi can be directly conditioned by technical factors, such as correct handling of the brush, movements of the wrist, angle of contact between the tip of the brush and the paper, and so forth. Qi in itself is invisible, but its effects and action are as evident and measurable as, for instance, the effects and action of electrical energy. Like electricity, it is without body or form, and yet its reality is physical: it can be stored or discharged; it pervades, informs, and animates all phenomena. Although to fully grasp this concept would require us to refer to Chinese philosophy and cosmology, its esthetic applications present universal relevance. Once more, the Chinese have analyzed more systematically and more deeply a phenomenon of which Western painters did not remain unaware: a painting must be invested with an inner cohesion that underlies forms and innervates the intervals between forms. In a mediocre painting, forms are separated by dead intervals, and blanks are negative spaces. But when a painting is charged with qi, there are exchanges of current that pass between the forms; their interaction makes the void vibrate. A painter should aim to turn his painting into a sort of energy field where forms constitute as many poles between which tensions are created; these tensions—invisible, yet active—ensure the unity and vital dynamism of the composition. All these basic notions have been explored by and experimented with by Paul Klee, for instance. What is perhaps one of the best descriptions of the role of qi was provided by André Masson without any reference to Chinese painting: "A great painting is a painting where intervals

are charged with as much energy as the figures which circum-
scribe them."*

It is in the art of painting that the concept of qi found some of
its most obvious applications; yet in literature it plays a role that
is no less important. Han Yu (768–824) described its operation
with a striking image: "Qi is like water, and words are like objects floating on the water. When the water reaches a sufficient
level, the objects, small and big, can freely move; such is the
relation between qi and words. When qi is at its fullness, both
the amplitude and the sound of the sentences reach a perfect
pitch."† As we can see, the qi of literature is essentially the same
as the qi of painting: in both arts, it is an energy that underlies
the work, endowing it with articulation, texture, rhythm, and
movement. (Flaubert, laboring on *Madame Bovary*, was precisely seeking to let this invisible yet active current pass through
his book, as it was only this inner circulation that could bring
breath and life to the words, sentences, and paragraphs and
make them cohere; as he himself wrote, one must feel in a book
"a long energy that runs from beginning to end without slack-
ening."‡)

It should be noted, incidentally, that the action of qi can be
observed nowhere more clearly than in these purely imagist
verses (two examples of which were given above), where syntax
completely disappears and grammatical connections dissolve.
There we see the fleet of words, all moorings having been cast
loose, which is set unanimously in motion; the swell, rocking
them on a common rhythm, alone ensures their cohesion.

---

* Quoted by D. Kahnweiler, *Juan Gris* (Paris: Gallimard, 1946), 188.

† On this question, see D. Pollard, "Ch'i in Chinese Literary Theory," in A. A. Rick-
ett, ed., *Chinese Approaches to Literature from Confucius to Liang Ch'i-ch'ao*
(Princeton, N.J.: Princeton University Press, 1978), 56.

‡ Quoted by Nadeau in Introduction to *Madame Bovary*, 8.

For any artist, whether a painter or a poet, it is thus imperative that he be able first and foremost to grasp and nurture qi, and to impart its energy to his own creation. If his works are not vested with this vital inspiration, if they "lack breath," all the other technical qualities they may present will remain useless. Conversely, if they are possessed of such inner circulation, they may even afford to be technically clumsy; no formal defect can affect their essential quality. Hence, also, the first task of a critic will be to gauge the intensity of qi expressed in any given work of art.

The unique emphasis put on the expression of qi has important consequences: originality and formal invention are not valued per se. So long as the artist is able to transmit qi, it is quite irrelevant whether the formal pretext of his work is original or borrowed. Theoretically, one can conceive of a copy that may be superior to its model, to the extent that it succeeds in injecting more qi into its borrowed composition.

Primacy of expression over invention is thus a fundamental aspect of Chinese esthetics. The best example can be found in calligraphy,* which—as everyone knows—is considered in China as *the* supreme art of the brush. No other art is more narrowly governed by formal and technical conventions, leaving less room to the artist's imagination and initiative: not only are cal-

---

* Or in music. A good introduction to this topic can be found in R. H. van Gulik, *The Lore of the Chinese Lute* (Tokyo: Tuttle, 1968). The melodic repertory of the zither is limited, although it presents extraordinarily rich variations and nuances of timbre: "The [zither] is not easy to appreciate, chiefly because its music is not primarily melodical. Its beauty lies not so much in the succession of notes as in each separate note in itself. 'Painting with sounds' might be a way to describe its essential quality. The timbre being thus of the utmost importance, there are very great possibilities of modifying the coloring of one and the same tone. In order to understand and appreciate this music, the ear must learn to distinguish subtle nuances: the same note, produced on a different string, has a different color; the same string when pulled by the forefinger or the middle finger of the right hand, has a different timbre. The technique by which these variations in timbre are effected is extremely complicated: of the vibrato alone, there exist no less than twenty-six varieties." (van Gulik, *The Lore of the Chinese Lute*, 1–2.)

ligraphers not allowed to invent the form of any written character,
but the number of brushstrokes and the very order in which the
brushstrokes must follow each other, are rigorously predeter-
mined. On the other hand, paradoxically, calligraphy is also the
art that can afford an individual with the greatest scope to display
in a direct and lyrical way his unique personality, mood, and
tempor, and all the subtle, intimate nuances of his sensibility.

A similar phenomenon is to be found in painting and in poetry.
For a layman, at first sight, Chinese painting may appear rather
limited and monotonous; landscapes, for instance, are invariably
built on a combination of mountains and rivers, organized on the
basis of a few set recipes. These stereotyped formulas are themselves filled with conventional elements—trees, rocks, clouds,
buildings, figures— whose treatment is standardized in painting
handbooks that are straightforward catalogues of forms. The
range of poetry is equally narrow: it uses a rigidly codified symbolic language, a set of ready-made images (the song of the cuc-
koo that makes the traveler feel homesick; the wild geese that
fail to bring news from the absent lover; the east wind with its
springtime connotations; the west wind and the funereal feelings
of autumn; mandarin ducks suggesting shared love; ruins of ancient monuments witnessing the impermanence of human endeavors; willow twigs exchanged by friends as a farewell present;
moon and wine; falling flowers; the melancholy of the abandoned
woman leaning on her balcony). In a sense, one could say that
Chinese poetry is made of a narrow series of clichés embroidered
upon a limited number of conventional canvases. And yet such
a definition, although it would be literally accurate, would nevertheless miss the point; a deaf man could as well describe a Bach
sonata for cello as a sequence of rubbings and scratchings effected upon four gut-strings stretched over an empty box.

Poetry is, of course, untranslatable by its very nature; in the
case of Chinese poetry, however, this impossibility is further
compounded with a basic misunderstanding. Here, indeed,

translation operates like a perverse screen that saves the chaff in order to eliminate the grain. What the translator offers to the reader's admiration is precisely the least admirable part of the poem: its subject matter (generally trite) and its images (borrowed, nine times out of ten, from a conventional catalogue and hence utterly devoid of originality). The specific quality of the poem necessarily escapes the translator, since (as is also the case with painting and calligraphy) *it does not reside in a creation of new signs, but in a new way of using conventional signs.* For a poet, the supreme art is to position, adjust, and fit together these well-worn images in such a way that, from their unexpected encounter, a new life might spark.

In this sense, one should say that in Chinese art, the emphasis is always on *interpretation* rather than on *invention.* "Interpretation" should be understood here in the musical sense of the word. Ivan Moravec, let us say, is not a lesser artist for not having himself composed the Chopin nocturnes that he interprets. And yet, it is through the very fidelity of his interpretation that he manages to express his own individuality and sensibility. It is his *creative* genius that is different from the one of Claudio Arrau, or of any other musician interpreting this same piece. *By narrowing the field of its invention, an art intensifies the quality of its expression*—or rather, it shifts creation from the first arena to the second. (Actually, this axiom has a validity that goes beyond Chinese esthetics: see, for instance, in modern European art the beginnings of Cubism. For Braque, Picasso, and Gris, the world suddenly seemed to shrink to the mere dimensions of a guitar, a newspaper, and a fruit dish—the very conventions that freed these artists from the need to define a new subject matter allowed them to concentrate entirely on the problem of elaborating a new language. Earlier, one mountain and twelve apples had already fulfilled the same function for Cézanne.)

For a painter or a poet, the question is not how to eliminate stereotypes, but how to handle them in such a way that, through the stereotypes, the "current" may flow. Under the efficient power of qi, a conventional mountain-and-water combination can then become a microcosmic creation, the worn-out image of falling flowers can turn into a poignant and universal metaphor of fate, and the old cliché of the abandoned woman on her balcony becomes an effective summing-up of the entire human condition.

THE POWER OF EMPTINESS

Earlier, we pointed out that in Chinese philosophy the Absolute only manifests itself "in hollow": only its absence can be circumscribed. We met a first important application of this conception in the precept that recommends the painter always reveal only half of his subject in order to better suggest its totality. Not only can the message reach its destination without having to be fully spelled out, but it is precisely because it is not fully spelled out that it can reach its destination. In this sense, the "blanks" in painting, the silences in poetry and music are active elements that bring a work to life.

There is something more important than a finished work of art: it is the spiritual process that preceded it and guided its execution. The poet Tao Yuanming (372–427) used to carry everywhere with him a zither without strings, on which he played mute music: "I only seek the meaning that lies at the heart of the zither. Why strain myself to produce sounds on the strings?"

The finished work is to the spiritual experience of the artist as the graph recorded by the seismograph is to an earthquake. What matters is the experience; the work itself is a mere accidental consequence, a secondary result, a visible (or audible) left-over—it is nothing but "the imprint left perchance in the snow by a wild swan." This is the reason why sometimes the ink of the brushstroke, the sound of the musical note are divested of part of their material substance; they are thinned out in order better to reveal the actual gesture that originates and underlies them. (To achieve this result in painting and calligraphy, the brushstroke is applied with an ink load that is deliberately insufficient; in this way, the ink mark is striated with "blanks" that show the inner dynamics of the stroke; this technique is called *fei bai*, which means "flying white." A similar effect is found in music, when the sound of the fingernail modulating the vibrato on the string becomes louder than the original sound of the note.)

Literature, too, has its "blanks." Sometimes they function as hinges for the composition; sometimes they enable the poem to suggest the existence of another poem that lies beyond words. To a degree, Western literature also knows these two uses of emptiness. A good illustration of the latter one was provided by Virginia Woolf when she presented Vita Sackville-West with what she called her best work—a splendidly bound volume, made purely of blank pages. As to emptiness used as a compositional device, Proust very subtly describes how Flaubert handled this technique: "To my mind, the most beautiful thing in *Sentimental Education* is not a sentence, it is a blank . . . [by which Flaubert finally] rids the narrative of all the deadwood of storytelling. He was thus the first writer who succeeded in giving it a musical quality."*

---

* M. Proust, "A propos du style de Flaubert," in *Contre Sainte-Beuve* (Paris: Pléiade, 1971), 595: "To my mind, the most beautiful thing in *Sentimental Education* is not a sentence, it is a blank. Flaubert has just described in many pages the minutest moves of Frédéric Moreau. Then he tells us that Frédéric sees a policeman charging with his sword against a rebel who falls dead: 'And Frédéric, openmouthed, recognized Sénécal.' Then, a 'blank,' a huge 'blank,' and without the slightest transition, suddenly time is not anymore measured in quarters of an hour but in years, in dozens of years; I copy again the last words I just quoted in order to show this extraordinary shift of speed for which there was no preparation:

And Frédéric, openmouthed, recognized Sénécal. He traveled. He came to know the melancholy of the steamboat, the cold awakening in the tent, etc. . . . ."

In turn, Proust's observation was well commented upon by Maurice Nadeau: "Proust noticed it: the 'blanks' in the narrative of *Sentimental Education* as well as in *Madame Bovary* are their supreme achievement. . . . At every subtle turn of Emma's fate, whenever a secondary narrative accompanies the main story, we encounter this 'unsaid.' The same current pervades objects and consciousness, the material world and the psychological world exchange their respective qualities; reality and the expression of reality merge into one single totality that rests upon 'the inner dynamics of style.' "* The Flaubertian notion of "inner dynamics of style" irresistibly calls to mind the Chinese concept of qi; it should be observed that it is precisely *emptiness* that provides the best conductor for this "current."

* Maurice Nadeau in Introduction to *Madame Bovary*, 15–16. Claude Roy made similar observations on Stendhal (*Stendhal par lui-même* [Paris: le Seuil, 1971], 47): "A novel by Stendhal is written in a way that is the exact opposite of nine out of ten of the great novelists who came before him. The narrative progresses as much through what is said as through what is omitted. There are two novels within *Red and Black*—the novel of the events that are printed, and the novel of the events that are eluded: the latter are no less important. One could write another version of Julien's story, simply by filling in all the blanks of the narrative. Just imagine another writer describing the first night which Julien spent with Mathilde: all the things he would have to write, Stendhal puts in a semicolon: 'Julien's prowess was equal to his happiness; "I cannot go down the ladder," he said to Mathilde when he saw the dawn appear. . . .' A semicolon alone accounts of a whole night, two lovers in each other's arms, their ecstasy, their mutual love-confessions, their pleasure, etc. In *Vanina Vanini*, the entire story ends with a two-minute scene that occupies three pages of dialogue. Then, two lines only: 'Vanina stood dumbfounded. She returned to Rome; and the newspaper is reporting that she just married Prince Savelli.' " Stendhal's latter quote is remarkably similar to the Flaubert passage that Proust admired so much (see previous note). Strange power of litotes! Because it relies on the reader's imagination, it is more effective than an explicit description. Claude Roy pursues: "What seems to us discretion on Stendhal's part appeared in his time as impudence. He shocked his readers, who felt that he was telling too much." Splendid illustration of the esthetic principle "less is more." If literature has its litotes, and painting its blanks, music also has its silences: it may be apposite to quote here Daniel Barenboim's warning to the musicians of his orchestra that they should carefully observe the pauses of a score: "Silence is the paper on which all music is written."

Void is the space where the poem-beyond-the-poem can develop; Chinese poetry has various devices to create it. Thus, for instance, at the beginning of the famous four-line poem by Wang Zhihuan describing the immense scenery that can be seen from a tower at the mouth of the Yellow River, the first two verses outline the widest possible horizon:

The sun sinks beyond the mountains
The Yellow River flows into the ocean . . .

At this point the reader feels that the poet has reached the utter limit of his vision; actually, the real function of these two verses is merely to tighten a spring whose sudden release, at the end of the poem, is going to launch the reader's imagination into the infinitely vaster spaces of the unseen:

However, if you wish to see a really huge scenery
Climb one more story!

The last verse is not a point of arrival, but a point of departure. This "trampoline effect" is often used by poets, especially in the four-line poems whose extreme compactness (the entire poem may have twenty syllables only) is thus prolonged with an infinite echo.

Another method consists in building the poem around a central core of emptiness, where a truth resides that cannot be approached or expressed. The traditional metaphor used for this purpose is that of the unsuccessful attempt to meet a hermit-sage who possesses the ultimate answer. The hermit's presence is real and near—it is attested by various clues, even by his direct messengers—and yet he himself remains invisible and unreachable. A good thousand years before Kafka's *Castle*, Jia Dao summarized this myth in a well-known four-line poem:

Under a pine tree, the boy-servant, having been asked where his
  master was,
Answers: "He went to collect medicinal herbs;
I only know that he is somewhere in this mountain.
Where? Mist hides everything."

Since the essential point is beyond words, a poem can only talk *beside* the subject—it describes a desire. Thus, in Tao Yuanming:

I built my hut among people
And yet their noise does not disturb me.
How is this possible, I ask you?
Solitude can be created by the mind, it is not a matter of distance.
Plucking chrysanthemums at the foot of the hedge,
I gaze toward the faraway mountains.
At dusk the mountain air is beautiful,
When birds are returning.
Truth is at the heart of all this:
I wish to express it, yet find no words.

The same theme found a new expression with Wang Wei:

In the evening of life, I am only fond of silence;
I do not care anymore for the business of the world.
Having measured my own limits,
I merely wish to return to my old forest.
The wind that blows in the pine trees plays with my belt.
In the mountain, I play the zither under the moon.
You ask what is the ultimate answer?
It is the song of a fisherman sailing back to shore.

Any work of art—poem, painting, piece of music—plays the part of a "fisherman's song": beyond the words, forms, and sounds that it borrows, it is a direct, intuitive experience of a reality that no discursive approach can embody.

In our time, the subtlest of all modern critics, Zhou Zuoren (1885–1968), summarized in one pithy sentence this living tradition of which he himself was a product: "All that can be spelled out is without importance."

This axiom—needless to say—is also valid for essays that deal with Chinese esthetics.

MADNESS OF
THE WISE:
RICCI IN CHINA

■   ■   ■   ■   ■

I n the sixteenth century, a Spanish missionary who had repeatedly failed in his attempts to enter China concluded that
such an endeavor was akin to trying to reach the moon. In
fact, reaching the moon proved to be a much easier task—and
also a far less interesting one. Whereas the exploration of our
dead satellite is a mere technological venture that can only yield
scientific data, a true spiritual encounter between the West and
China not only would provide mankind with a deeper understanding and knowledge of itself, it might even ensure that our
planet enjoys a civilized future.

The unique fascination that China exerts upon all those who

come into contact with her can in a way be compared to the attraction between the opposite sexes: although China is often described with a florid imagery that suggests romance, magic, and mystery, its fascination rests upon a basic and obvious fact. From a Western point of view, China is simply the other pole of the human mind. All the other great cultures are either dead (Egypt, pre-Columbian America, and so on), or too exclusively absorbed by the problem of surviving in extreme conditions (primitive cultures), or too close to us (Islamic cultures, India) to present a contrast as total, a revelation as complete, an "otherness" as challenging, an originality as illuminating as China. It is only when we contemplate China that we can become exactly aware of our own identity and that we begin to perceive which part of our heritage truly pertains to universal humanity, and which part merely reflects Indo-European idiosyncrasies.

In a sense, the Catholic missionaries who brought the Gospel to the four corners of the earth in the wake of the great journeys of discovery during the Renaissance should have been well equipped to meet the challenge of the Chinese cultural revelation. They knew that all men were equally God's children, and since they had already been able to witness how, by an accident of history, the Jewish God had come to borrow Roman garb, they should have been quite prepared to accept that he might now adopt with equal ease a clothing even more exotic.

Unfortunately, most of them failed to match their belief in the universality of human nature with an awareness of the relativity of their own culture. Since Westerners had become Christian, they generally assumed that, to be a Christian, one ought to become a Westerner. In practice, Asians who wished to be baptized first had to be turned into honorary Spaniards or Portuguese. Evangelization became a by-product of colonization.

The consequences of this attitude could be nowhere more disastrous than in China, since the Ming dynasty by the sixteenth century had developed an equally dangerous misconception. Originally the Chinese order had been conceived as a mere stepping-stone, a mediation between the individual and the world in the pursuit of a universal humanist harmony. Still, for various geopolitical factors and historical reasons, the Chinese eventually found it more convenient to decide that, after all, China *was* the world, and in order to prevent reality from upsetting such a view, they had the outside world carefully and effectively fenced out.

Thus, whereas Western missionaries were ascribing universal relevance to their particular values (the "God-speaks-Latin" syndrome), China denied that the world actually extended beyond her own borders (the "Great-Wall" syndrome). In such a situation, the early missionaries were naturally doomed to be ignored.

It finally fell to an Italian Jesuit, Matteo Ricci (1552–1610), to effect the first breakthrough and implant Christianity in China. The story of his endeavors, of the intellectual exchanges and the friendships that he established with illustrious members of the Chinese scholarly elite, the subsequent growth of a Chinese Church and the dramatic setbacks that were to endanger it in later centuries, constitutes one of the most intriguing episodes in the history of civilization.

By modern standards, Ricci's life was a heroic adventure. In the sixteenth century, to sail to the other end of the world was a risky undertaking. Anyway, in the best of circumstances, the missionaries who survived this ordeal were not supposed to ever return home—usually they would live and die in the remote countries where they had been sent. All the emotional and spiritual links that they retained with their relatives, friends, superiors, and colleagues in Europe were entirely dependent upon the vagaries of mail that could take years to reach its destination—if it reached it at all. A lifetime of hardships, trials, and dangers of all kinds awaited the lonely priests on strange and sometimes

hostile shores. Yet if Ricci's saintliness, courage, faith, resilience, and resourcefulness may appear superhuman to us today,
these virtues were by no means exceptional among the early Jesuit missionaries. What distinguished him from his colleagues
was a unique combination of subtler qualities that enabled him
to succeed where they had repeatedly failed.

He was a gentleman and a scholar. He was highly cultured—
in both literary and scientific fields—and had exquisite manners.
He was a man of God, but he was also very shrewd, a born dip-
lomat, tactful and inventive, able to gauge situations, to judge
and handle people. He was a great artist in human relations—
an art that Chinese society had brought to perfection. Being Italian (from the Papal Domain) he had inherited the best of a glorious and sophisticated cultural tradition, without having to carry
the burden of imperial-nationalist hangovers from which Spaniards and Portuguese were seldom free. For the Chinese (as for
the French), any new idea, in order to be taken seriously, must
not only be expressed in their own language, but it must also be
expressed with literary elegance.

Ricci was able to meet this requirement because his mastery
of Chinese language and culture was not merely the product of
an intellectual effort, but also the result of a living commitment.
He discovered that in order to convert China to Christianity he
should first convert himself to China. The refinement of his mind
combined with a true genius for friendship won him an amazing
popularity among Chinese intellectual circles. Another Jesuit
who was his companion described the impression he made:

Incredible is the reputation which good Father Ricci enjoys
among the Chinese and the extent to which he is visited by important personages and esteemed throughout the whole empire of
China. They say that there cannot be another man in Europe
equal to him. And when we say that others are more gifted than
he, they cannot believe it. In truth, he captivates everyone by

the graciousness and suavity of his manners, by his conversation and by the solid virtue which his life exhibits.

The accuracy of this description is confirmed by an unimpeachable Chinese witness. Li Zhi, one of the most original Chinese thinkers of all times, a flamboyant figure and also a man of unbending integrity, was fascinated by Ricci's personality and visited him several times. Later on, he reported in a letter to a friend:

Ricci has read all our classics. He speaks our language to perfection, writes our characters and knows how to conform to our social usages. He is a truly remarkable man. He is utterly refined, but his appearance is of great simplicity. In the middle of a noisy and boisterous gathering of people where everyone is shouting and arguing, he maintains an imperturbable composure. He is the most extraordinary man I ever met. Other people either are too rigid or too lax; either they wish to make a display of their wit, or they are dull—they all are his inferiors. However, I still do not understand why he came to China. I really cannot believe that he would actually want to substitute his own doctrine for the Confucian teachings. This would be too absurd! He must have some other purpose.

Li Zhi unwittingly pinpointed the paradox of Ricci's enterprise, its essential absurdity. Ricci himself, whose profound faith was matched with an equal dose of astuteness, was fully aware of the problem. From the beginning, he saw (to borrow the words of one of his modern biographers, G. H. Dunne) that "the primary task was not to multiply baptisms, but to win for Christianity an accepted place in Chinese life." In order to achieve this objective, he chose to proceed "*suave modo*," as he said, laying the strategic plans that were to secure his success first in Southern China, then in Nanking, and finally in Peking: "I do not think that we shall establish a church, but instead a room for

discussion and we will say Mass privately in another chapel, because one preaches more effectively and with greater fruit here
through conversations than through formal sermons."

"Formal sermons" were not all that would have prematurely
exposed his preposterous design to convert China (so preposterous in fact that Li Zhi simply could not believe that a man of his
intelligence would seriously contemplate such a project). The
Christian doctrine was itself too shocking to bear being directly
disclosed to unprepared minds. A long historical familiarity with
Christianity has numbed our imagination; we hardly apprehend
anymore the full horror and scandal that lie at its very heart. On
his way to Peking, where he had finally been promised an imperial audience, Ricci was arrested by a greedy official who,
looking for loot, had his luggage searched. The search produced
a crucifix that, being in the hyperrealistic Spanish style of the
time, truly terrified the official. Whoever would travel with such
a gruesome object, he thought, must be practicing some kind of
evil voodoo—maybe the life of the emperor himself could be en-
dangered by these sinister rituals.

Summoned to provide an explanation, Ricci did not follow the
advice of the ebullient and not-too-subtle Spanish Jesuit who was
traveling with him, and who would have liked to put up a heroic
show; the Spaniard, indeed, wished to proclaim that "This was
the true God, creator of heaven and earth, whom all the world
must adore; who for our sins and to give us life, died and then
rose from the dead, and ascended into heaven." Instead Ricci
wisely refrained from disclosing the exact identity of the Cruci-
fied and merely said, "This was a great saint who had wished to
suffer for us the pain of the Cross, and that for this reason we
made sculptured and painted representations of him in order to
have him before our eyes so that we may be grateful for so great
a benefit."

Some zealots reproached him for his prudence and diplomatic

flexibility, as they would also reproach him for some of his associations; Ricci sometimes pursued friendships for friendship's sake with endearing rakes who offered no hope for conversion, since they felt unable to amend their way of life (though some of them finally converted and became admirable Christians). Actually, Ricci could have invoked authoritative precedents. Wasn't he spontaneously imitating Christ's conviviality? Zealots tend to forget that at Cana, for example, when Jesus began his public activity, the first thing he did was to provide more wine to revelers who had already drunk more than their share; and in choosing his friends, he too gave respectable people much cause for scandal.

The psychological observation made by Claude Roy in another context—"I do not believe in what my friend believes, but I believe in my friend"—could perhaps apply here to some extent, and help us to understand how so many Chinese intellectuals could be attracted to Christianity mostly because of Ricci's exceptional personality. Of course, to describe their attitude in such terms should by no means detract from the value and meaning of their conversions. Again, Christ himself did not proceed differently: for a long time, he postponed revealing the essential part of his doctrine, knowing all too well that it would prove a stumbling block to most of his followers. After he finally told a gathering of enthusiastic supporters that they would have to eat his flesh and drink his blood, nearly everyone left him, in shock and disgust. At that juncture only a tiny group of friends remained with him, not because they had a better understanding of what he meant (actually they felt equally dismayed by his aberrant suggestion), but simply because they loved him.

Still, after Ricci's death, there was a strong backlash. In their eagerness to bridge the enormous gap between two traditions that were so utterly alien to each other, the Jesuits had often been tempted to build hastily upon artificial similarities—for instance, the Chinese concept of "Heaven" was all too quickly assimilated to the Christian God. For their part missionaries were all the more tempted to point to such parallels as the strong common ground that they found between Christian and Confucian ethics. Moreover, at first the warm and charismatic personality of Ricci himself unwittingly contributed to mask some fundamental differences. After his death, however, an awareness of the seriousness of the doctrinal difficulties began to develop on both sides. The concepts of creation, fall, incarnation, and redemption all occasioned considerable problems of communication. More essential, the idea of a transcendent, personal God could hardly be reconciled with the Chinese conception of an immanent force of cosmic transformation.

Ricci accurately saw—and it remains his most momentous contribution—that the question of how China could become Christian was first the question of how Christianity should become Chinese. In practice, however, in spite of all his efforts, his theology remained inevitably encumbered with a number of narrowly Western notions, which, once transported into a Chinese context, appeared utterly arbitrary, or presented insoluble problems of translation. For instance, Western ontology is entirely predicated upon a bizarre linguistic accident that is found only in Indo-European languages, where the same expression, "to be," happens simultaneously to fulfill functions and meanings (essence, existence, identity) that normally are sharply differentiated in most other languages. Thus, when translated into Chinese, Thomas Aquinas's ontological proof of the existence of God (not to mention Hamlet's soliloquy!) appears merely to be a pun that doesn't work. Medieval scholastic philosophy is a monument as sublime as the great gothic cathedrals of Europe, but it is equally unfit for transplantation. This could hardly have been perceived, of course, four hundred years ago.

The anti-Christian reaction that developed in late Ming and

early Qing time was at first purely intellectual. It was soon to be aggravated by the rivalries and quarrels among the various missionary societies; and these, in turn, provoked a political reaction, and China came close to rejecting Christianity altogether. After the sorry interlude of the nineteenth century, when the new growth of the Church was directly tied to the encroachments of Western imperialism, the twentieth century finally witnessed a return to Ricci's original vision: the development of a Catholic Church that would be faithful both to the successors of Peter and to its own Chinese identity.

The establishment of the Communist regime was soon followed by a cruel persecution of all Christians. Catholics fared worst because of their fidelity to the spiritual authority of the Pope. Nearly all the Chinese Jesuits were thrown into jails and labor camps as early as the fifties; a few were briefly released during the phony "liberalization" that followed Mao's death, but now most of them have already been rearrested. Ricci did not labor in vain after all. Today, the unwavering faith of his spiritual sons bears testimony to the saintliness of Chinese Catholicism and already heralds its future blossoming. For the last thirty-six years, China under Marxism-Leninism was subjected to the tyranny of a Western idea gone mad—paradoxically, this very ordeal seems to have given her citizens a genuine and secret thirst for the real thing. Young people who were force-fed Communist ideology are now developing a new curiosity and desire for religion.

The Jesuits' interpretation of Chinese culture, the Chinese response to Christianity, and the philosophical misunderstandings that developed on both sides are a complex and fascinating topic. It was the subject of a masterly study by the leading French sinologist and historian Jacques Gernet, *Chine et Christianisme: Action et réaction.** The book is based on primary sources—early

* (Paris: Gallimard, 1982)

Jesuit reports, original Chinese pamphlets for and against Christianity. It is a work of penetrating intelligence and a model of scholarship. Nonspecialist readers should enjoy it without any difficulty, as it is written with clarity and elegance and addresses a subject that should be of immediate concern to any thinking person. It is hoped that such a fundamental work shall soon be translated into English.

On Ricci himself, there were at least two readable and competent biographies. Vincent Cronin's *The Wise Man from the West** is good but geared toward a more popular audience; G. H. Dunne's *Generation of Giants: The Story of the Jesuits in China in the Last Decades of the Ming Dynasty*† is better; it provides scholarly information as well as stimulating interpretations.

Now there is Jonathan Spence's *The Memory Palace of Matteo Ricci*.‡ I confess that I find it difficult to assign it a precise place alongside these earlier studies. The problem that Gernet analyzed is entirely ignored by Spence (strangely enough, Gernet's book is not even mentioned in Spence's bibliography). This is a serious failing. Compared with the two earlier biographers, moreover, Spence does not really provide new information, but he presents it in a very original arrangement. Whereas the other writers narrated Ricci's story in a conventional sequence, i.e., beginning with the beginning and ending with the end, Spence tells it in jumbled fashion. Although his life is divided into nine chapters, Ricci dies as early as chapter 5—a chapter that is also devoted to his early education. Later chapters deal with other aspects of his activity and earlier chapters are concerned with later episodes, which themselves are not set in chronological— or logical—order. The method is new, and somewhat perplexing.

---

* (London: Hart Davis, 1955)

† (Notre Dame, Ind.: University of Notre Dame Press, 1962)

‡ (New York: The Viking Press, 1984)

If you wish to check again some specific passage that caught your attention on your first reading, but you forgot to make a particular note of the page number, there is no hope that you will ever find it, unless you read the whole book all over—a rather inconvenient procedure.

Professor Spence has already written several brilliant books. In a sense, he is the Picasso of Chinese studies: he invented the sinological collage. He scavenges in the junkyard of history, retrieves odd bits and pieces, and fits them into amazing new shapes; with deft scissors, he cuts scraps of information here and there and pastes them together to create surprising, fresh patterns. Thus the formal pretext on which the complex architecture of this *Memory Palace* is essentially based was borrowed from one passage in a little treatise on mnemotechnics, which Ricci wrote in Chinese (*Xiguo Jifa*, chapter 2). Ricci was endowed with a phenomenal memory and used to entertain his Chinese friends with his astounding skills. The audience would provide him with a series of characters—hundreds of them, written on a piece of paper in meaningless, random sequence. Ricci would read this nonsensical list once and then repeat it from memory, in its exact original order, from beginning to end, and then again from end to beginning. Such a talent was immensely valued among Chinese scholars, as memory skills played a crucial part in the civil-service examinations. Hence Ricci was constantly pressed to explain and teach his technique, and eventually he wrote a small treatise on the subject in Chinese. For the sake of demonstration, in one of the many examples that are provided in his booklet, Ricci proposes an arbitrary sequence of four disconnected words and shows how memory can link them together and retain an imaginary grasp upon them. These words in turn were used by Spence to determine the basic successive themes of Ricci's biography. But this original idea is of doubtful practical value. Would a biography of Pascal gain much by duplicating the formal structure of his *Treatise on Atmospheric Pressure* or of his *Experiments on the Vacuum?* Furthermore, the words that in Spence's study come to occupy such a key position were, by definition, purely random and meaningless from Ricci's point of view. With such a method, we could as well try to extrapolate the decisive dates of Professor Spence's life from the digits of his phone number. Or he himself might attempt to compose his next historical essay in acrostic verses.

Having imposed such extraordinary manneristic constraints upon himself, the fact that he still managed to write a book that remains readable, and even attractive in some respects, represents no mean achievement—but, of course, Professor Spence's culture and literary skills are considerable. Still, his very talent may be his own worst enemy. The life of Ricci is so gripping a story that even a pedestrian scribbler could write a most magnificent book, were he simply to tell it straightforwardly from A to Z. It took a very clever man indeed to reduce it to the proportions of a mere literary game.

When Picasso (to go back to our original comparison) turned a broken bicycle into a Minotaur, or a gas-stove tap into a Venus, we marveled at his ability to make monuments out of junk. It would be unfair to say that Professor Spence does the exact opposite. Still, one deplores that he wasted such noble and inspiring material in the fabrication of what is, after all, a rather quaint *bibelot.*

PEREGRINATIONS
AND PERPLEXITIES
OF PÈRE HUC

■   ■   ■   ■   ■

T he fame of Father Huc is essentially based upon the remarkable journey that he made with his superior, Father Gabet, from 1844 to 1846, across the border regions of the
Chinese empire, up to Tibet. His narrative of this expedition,
first published in 1850 under the title *Souvenirs d'un voyage dans
la Tartarie et le Thibet*, enjoyed an enormous success both with
general readers and among literary circles.*

* Half a century later, Leon Bloy noted in his journal that reading Huc remained for
him "a supreme resource" whenever he felt that he was "dying of boredom" (L.
Bloy, *Le Vieux de la Montagne* [Paris: Mercure de France, 1963], 33, entry dated

The triumphant success of his first book gave Huc the idea of pursuing this new-found writing career; meanwhile, he had settled back in France and expressed the wish to leave his religious congregation (the council of the Lazarist Order was eventually to accept his resignation in 1855). An attempt to further exploit his original success resulted in the publication in 1854 of *L'Empire chinois*. Unlike *Souvenirs*, which remained constantly in print and was translated into several languages, the second book was reprinted twice only (in 1857 and 1862) and subsequently fell into an oblivion that today seems rather unfair.

Of course, strictly speaking, *L'Empire chinois* was hardly more than an artificially inflated postscript appended to the huge epic of the earlier book. Its ambitious title could not disguise the thinness of its actual contents, nor could the phony scholarship of its endless quotations and digressions substitute for a relative lack of substance. The most sensational adventures of the journey had already been described in the first volume—how the two intrepid Frenchmen, after crossing mysterious and inaccessible regions, reached Lhasa, only to be expelled finally from Tibet on the in-

February 1, 1908). Fifty years earlier, his old master Barbey d'Aurevilly had been one of the enthusiastic critics who applauded the first publication of the book. Huc's impact was far-reaching. For instance, one of Baudelaire's famous prose poems (*Le Spleen de Paris*, XVI, "L'Horloge": "Les Chinois voient l'heure dans l'oeil des chats . . .") was directly developed from a passage of *L'Empire chinois*. The success of his first book, however, was not exactly of a kind that could satisfy the author's ambition. As Philippe-Henri d'Orléans has observed: "His narrative was considered as a mere entertainment. Readers ignored the informative—and hence, factual—side of the book, to focus upon its extraordinary aspects. His amazing stories were taken for pure products of his imagination. His book was given to children to read in the same fashion as today we give them Jules Verne's novels. According to the English writer Yule, a bishop—though he was a missionary—apologized one day for having such a 'piece of fiction' on his desk." (*Le Père Huc et ses critiques* [Paris: Calmann-Lévy, 1893], 3.) An English translation by William Hazlitt (*Travels in Tartary, Thibet and China*) was published in 1851, and reprinted in 1928 with a new introduction by Paul Pelliot.

itiative of the Chinese minister, who suspected them of being spies. In contrast to the dramatic and exotic materials presented in the first book, *L'Empire chinois* merely covers the last four relatively uneventful months of what had been a two-year expedition. The thread is picked up at the point where the two missionaries find themselves back in China after their expulsion from Tibet, and the narrative describes their return to Guangzhou (Canton) across the provinces of Sichuan, Hubei, Jiangxi, and Guangdong. Naturally, after all the tribulations experienced by our holy adventurers in the steppes of Tartary and in the Tibetan snows—and from which Huc had extracted with much talent his earlier best-seller—it appeared to the author that the relative banality of this provincial journey in a peaceful and well-ordered empire could hardly justify by itself the writing of a second book. Hence he found it necessary to compound his marvelously direct and vivid observations with a ponderous apparatus of fanciful scholarship, and with a bric-a-brac of endless and irrelevant quotations. This method in turn enabled him to give his book the majestic and misleading title *L'Empire chinois*, whereas something like "A four-month journey across four Chinese provinces" would have been much closer to reality. This unfortunate padding did not help him in the eyes of serious readers. Thus, for instance, a great scholar like Paul Pelliot, who wrote two essays on Huc, only paid attention to *Souvenirs*. He never bothered to comment on *L'Empire chinois;* its direct observations, which fascinate us so much today, were not of great interest for him, since they were concerned with an everyday China which, for Pelliot, who first went to China in 1900, was familiar and ordinary (life in the Chinese hinterlands had not changed much since Huc's time); as for the ersatz sinology that overloaded the book, it could only inspire him with this conclusion: "On Chinese history, no scholar would ever dream to seek reliable information from Huc."

Huc wrote still a third book, *Le Christianisme en Chine, en Tartarie et au Thibet.** This time he really had no more new tricks in his bag. If we leave aside the personal anecdotes that he had already told more successfully elsewhere, the book has nothing to offer but pages and pages of tedious quotations and unsound scholarship bordering on plagiarism. The only interest results from the fact that it sadly illustrates a certain type of missionary mentality in the colonial period. It also marks the sorry conclusion of the author's personal evolution. In his youth, Huc had been committed to generous liberal ideas, but at the end of his career he was to volunteer advice to Napoléon III, aggressively pushing for the French conquest of Indochina in the name of a lunatic and sinister theory according to which the God of the Bible had entrusted the white race with a right and duty to rule over the whole world.

Le Christianisme en Chine shall remain better forgotten; *L'Empire chinois,* however, is well worth reading again after more than a hundred years of oblivion. It is not merely a matter of acknowledging Huc's literary merits; these already were given full recognition, thanks to the constant popularity of *Souvenirs,* which occupies a prominent position among the splendid French travelogues of the nineteenth century. The specific interest of the second book resides in the fact that it still can answer some timely questions concerning both the problem of China and the problem of the Western perception of China. Whereas *Souvenirs* has somehow drifted further away from us, inasmuch as it described a world that does not exist anymore, *L'Empire chinois* illustrates some permanent aspects of China, as well as her genuine areas of change, and for this reason the book remains strikingly relevant today.

---

* 4 vols. (Paris: Gaume Frères, 1857–58). An English translation, *Christianity in China, Tartary and Tibet,* was published in London (Longman, Brown, Green, Longman and Roberts, 1857).

For the West, the problem of China is first the problem of how we know China. No observer approaches her safely; as he thinks he is describing her, he may actually be revealing his own secret fantasies—and in this sense, whoever talks about China talks about himself. Naturally, the fantasy element is always in inverse proportion to the amount of factual knowledge the observer may possess. With Huc, the wealth of firsthand experience acts as a mighty counterweight to his private obsessions and prejudices; yet we must first be aware of these in order to make good use of his testimony.

THE OTHER TRAVELER

Huc was truculent, colorful, exuberant, and boastful. With his boisterous personality, he nearly eclipsed his companion, Father Gabet, who seems to have been possessed of an evangelical zeal of a much deeper quality. Reading Huc, one might easily assume that Gabet was merely a humble assistant to our flamboyant adventurer. Actually Gabet—who was the older of the two—was the leader of the expedition, and Huc's superior in the religious hierarchy. One wants to know more about him, but as he seems to have been modest and retiring, his actual features remain somewhat blurred.* What is known about him can be summarized in a few words.

---

* M. Gindre, vice-president of the Agriculture, Sciences, and Arts Society of Poligny, has written a short essay on him: *Biographie de Mgr Gabet, de Nevy-sur-Seille (Jura)* (probably privately published by the author in Poligny, in 1867). The concentrated stupidity of this little monograph would have hypnotized Flaubert! Its most noteworthy contribution consists of a collection of purple metaphors and cretinous clichés, for which even the most superb pages of *Dictionnaire des idées re-*

Joseph Gabet was born in 1808 in the Jura. He sailed for China as a Lazarist missionary in 1835. He spent several years in Manchuria and Northern China. Having been entrusted with the task of establishing a new mission in Mongolia, he chose Huc as his traveling companion and started in 1844 on a daring journey that had ill-defined objectives. The general idea was to effect an initial survey of the potential that these largely unknown regions could present for evangelization. The two missionaries stayed for some time in Gansu, in a Lamaist monastery. Modifying their plans, they veered toward the southwest, aiming for Lhasa, which, contrary to what Huc was to write later, had not been the original goal of their expedition. Between Kuku-nor and Lhasa they had a very rough time, and Gabet nearly died. The two travelers eventually reached Lhasa at the end of 1848. The Tibetans proved to be most hospitable; the two companions had already set up a small chapel and intended to start preaching the Gospel, when the Chinese minister, suspecting them of being secret agents attempting to detach Tibet from the Chinese sphere of influence, engineered their expulsion. At the end of a journey across Southern China (which is described in *L'Empire chinois*) the two Lazarists finally reached Guangzhou in September 1846. From there they went to Macau, where their respective ways finally parted. Gabet went directly back to Europe in order to attempt—without success—to defend in Rome the interests of the Lazarist mission against the territorial encroachments of its pious competitor, the Foreign Missions Society.

çues are no match. For instance, in order to say that local people cultivate wheat and grapes, Gindre writes: "Blond Ceres and florid Bacchus compete for the inhabitants' hands." Horses are "solipeds"; Rome, "the city of the ancient masters of the known *orbis*"; Marseille, "the antique Phocean metropolis"; they had a good sleep: "Morpheus poured for them a generous concoction of his most soporific pavots"; medical advice: "the oracle of Epidaurus"; and so on. Yet, on the subject of Gabet himself, the glittering verbal diarrhea of the vice-president of the Agriculture, Sciences, and Arts Society of Poligny is finally not much more informative than the disconcerting silence of Huc.

Gabet's health had been badly shaken by the trials of his epic journey. As the doctors had strongly advised against his return to a cold climate, his superiors sent him to the tropics, where the heat killed him in no time. In 1848 he had been appointed as chaplain to a convent of German nuns in Brazil; having already learned Manchu, Chinese, Mongol, and Tibetan, he thus had the opportunity to apply himself to the study of German and Portuguese. Pelliot hints at a conflict that pitted him against his superiors and eventually resulted in a decision of the council of the Lazarists "to notify his expulsion from the congregation." This decision could not take effect as, meanwhile, Gabet had died of yellow fever in March 1853, near Rio de Janeiro. He was forty-five years old.

When one considers how closely the two travelers had been associated during their long expedition, it is somewhat disconcerting to note that Gabet remains practically invisible in Huc's narrative. This is particularly true of *L'Empire chinois*, in which Gabet's name is mentioned only *once* in the entire book, at the very end, where, having heard the news of his death, Huc perfunctorily evokes in three lines their past association. It would be perfectly idle to conjecture on the difficulties that might have crept into their relations; only one thing is obvious—one could hardly conceive of two personalities more utterly dissimilar. Gabet's coolheadedness and reserve were in complete contrast to the loquacity of his ebullient colleague, whose exuberance succeeded at once in monopolizing public attention. Pelliot observed accurately: "Huc's marvelously lively narrative pushed into the shadows the figure of his companion, who was also his elder and his leader. It seems that Huc endeavored immediately to occupy the center of the stage. As early as October 1846, as the travelers had just arrived, our consul in Macau speaks already of 'MM. Huc et Gabet.' Current usage followed the same order. It takes an effort for us today to reestablish their proper hierarchy and to say: 'Gabet and Huc.' "

During his stay in Europe, Gabet wrote a report titled "A Survey on the State of the China Missions, Presented to the Holy Father, Pope Pius IX."* This small monograph of eighty-one pages is of considerable interest and reveals the exceptional personality of its author. Gabet exhibits toward Chinese cultural values a deep respect of which most of his missionary colleagues—beginning with Huc!—were generally incapable. Furthermore, he displays rare courage and clearsightedness in the diagnosis that he draws of the sorry state of the missions in China, and also in the bold remedies he prescribes. Actually, his ideas were so far ahead of the time that they were not even opposed—they were totally ignored! It took eighty years before another intrepid priest, Father Vincent Lebbe, rediscovered these prophetic views and had them progressively accepted by the Church at the end of a long and painstaking struggle.

Gabet's report reads like a stark statement of bankruptcy. According to him, the missionary endeavor in China had essentially failed. Neither the missionaries' goodwill nor their material resources should be blamed for this dismal situation. Three main factors could explain why the efforts to Christianize China had achieved practically nothing. First, quarrels and rivalries among different missionary congregations paralyzed their activity and were a source of scandal for the nonbelievers; second, there were not enough Chinese priests, as the European priests were reluctant to train them, to trust them, and to treat them as their equals; and, third, missionaries had an insufficient knowledge of Chinese language and culture, and this prevented their preaching from being taken seriously. The two latter points are especially remarkable, as they show an ability to relinquish Eurocentric perspectives and to become open to Chinese values.

* Gabet ("Coup d'oeil sur l'état des missions de Chine, presenté au Saint Père le Pape Pie IX" [Poissy, France: 1948]).

This attitude is in contrast with the missionary mentality of the time, which, being closely associated with the colonial conquest, eventually attempted to justify its activity through the alleged superiority of Western civilization. Gabet wrote:

The Chinese have been able to preserve their empire during four thousand years; thousands of years ago they already possessed various artifacts and inventions that modern Europe proudly believed it had itself discovered, such as printing, gunpowder, the compass, silk-spinning, and weaving, the decimal system applied to various weights and measures, and many other things. How can the Europeans still dare to say that the Chinese nation is inferior to them in intelligence? The Chinese have ancient classics full of the deepest wisdom. . . . In these books, one finds worthy traditions and philosophical insights that are far superior to the entire intellectual production of our own pagan antiquity. Furthermore, they had the good sense to apply these excellent doctrines to the actual practice of government, which shows that they are wiser than the Europeans. . . . Even though they are pagans, the Chinese have established hospitals for orphans, for the old and the sick; they have welfare offices where food is freely provided to the destitute, and medicines to the sick. Along the highways, one finds shelters that have been erected for the free use of travelers. How could one dare to say that a nation which shows such enlightenment, generosity, and wisdom, even though it is still pagan, would not be able, once it is touched by our Redemptor's grace, to present as many resources for the development of a native clergy as any European nation?

The originality and prescience of these views shall be better appreciated once they are compared with Huc's opinions, which usually reflected the missionary and colonial prejudices common in the nineteenth century.

GASCON AND LAZARIST

Huc was born in 1813 in Caylus, the son of an army officer. He was endowed with all the braggadocio that is conventionally attributed to the natives of his province, and possessed, it seems, a secret envy for his father's saber. One often feels that a zouave uniform would have fit him better than a cassock. Having gone directly from the pious and sheltered little world of the Petit Séminaire of Toulouse to the Lazarist congregation in Paris, he may have mistaken an adolescent exaltation for a religious vocation. Actually, his superiors seem to have entertained some misgivings on this subject; he alone, of his entire class, had to delay his final vows by two years, since "he did not give full satisfaction in some respects." His sincerity cannot be questioned, but his spirituality appears rather shallow. In his writings, there is always an odd contrast between the dull conventionality of the edifying religious comments he feels obliged to introduce here and there, and the juicy and pungent flavor of all his secular observations. This puzzling ventriloquy seems to betray the coexistence in him of two different men; besides the ecclesiastical character he had had to impersonate since the Petit Séminaire, one sees a bold and flamboyant adventurer progressively emerging from his journeys and trials. As a young missionary he had been able to reconcile for a while these two different natures in one heroic dream of martyrdom: on his arrival in China, he asked that he be allowed to wear the priestly garments of his colleague Perboyre who had just been executed in Wuchang, so as to mark a determination to follow his example. And yet, five years later, our former candidate for martyrdom had gone quite a long way. Just look at him: dressed in fanciful, self-designed robes whose colors breached an imperial privilege, he is traveling across China with devilish cheek, pretending, cheating, wringing illegal advantages with a superb mixture of arrogance and cunning.

The glib tongue of a soldier of fortune from Gascony seems to have imperceptibly replaced the stoic humility that one would have expected from a follower of Christ. Huc believed that "with the Chinese, you can never afford to show the slightest weakness; you must always keep them with an iron hand." Hence, toward the local authorities, he always adopted a policy of systematic impudence. For instance, his greatest pleasure was to abash, insult, and ridicule high officials in front of their subordinates; he refused to kneel in front of a viceroy as ceremony prescribed. If occasionally he was served a poor meal, he would at once reassert his authority by ordering a first-class banquet at the expense of the local prefect. By sheer bluff he managed to invade the residence of a provincial governor. He usurped the chair of a judge in a tribunal, took over the proceedings, and turned to his own advantage all the solemn apparatus of the court of justice. The Reverend Father had in him the making of a magnificent crook; the fact that some of his improvisations reached epic proportions and were theoretically dedicated to God's greatest glory did not prevent them from looking very much like swindles. Moreover, the cynical cheerfulness with which he narrated them should have made his book really unfit for pious reading at mealtimes in convents; it reminds us more of the picaresque adventures of a witty scoundrel, and indeed, in this connection, a perceptive critic* has made a good parallel with Benvenuto Cellini's *Autobiography*.

When, halfway into the last leg of their journey, the Chinese authorities began to treat him and Gabet with less respect, he made inquiries and discovered that a saintly Spanish priest who had preceded them on the same road had spoiled the business for all his missionary colleagues by meekly letting himself be put

* Hubert Durt, "Le Voyage en Orient dans la littérature romantique," a lecture given in 1974 at the Institut Franco-Japonais in Kyōto.

in chains and dragged like a sheep from Wuchang to Guangzhou: "The good Spanish father, who had, I confess, more resignation and patience than us, had allowed the people of Wuchang to adopt an attitude that could become harmful for us."

Huc immediately proceeded to set the matter straight with breathtaking audacity. When he finally reached the very spot where the unfortunate Perboyre had been executed—Perboyre, whose example he had dreamed of emulating a few years earlier!—his boisterous energy seemed hardly compatible with the gentle and humble disposition that should be expected from a candidate for martyrdom: "We crossed the square where venerable Perboyre had been strangled; we were going to the very tribunal where he had been cruelly tortured and sentenced to death. Nothing could allow us to hope for a similar fate, for such a glorious end. However, these memories of constancy and courage intoxicated our souls and inspired us with indomitable energy, not in order to die—we were not worthy—but in order to live, as we believed it was our right."

He had an amazing resilience, a capacity always to land on his feet; his initiative was never short of inspiration, or his glibness short of breath. He inaugurates in literature the stereotype of the French traveler—half hero, half con man, brave, chivalrous, cheerful, and jingoistic. With his inexhaustible resourcefulness, high spirits, and foolhardiness, he is the spiritual father of Passepartout.*

Huc had arrived in China in 1841, six years later than Gabet. After their journey to Tibet, while Gabet returned directly to Europe, Huc stayed in Macau until 1849, then traveled for some time in Northern China; he eventually settled back in France in

---

* Jules Verne probably read Huc when he was a young man. Anyway, his imagination was struck by the Lazarists. In *Five Weeks in a Balloon*, for instance, the heroic missionary whom the explorers save from the hands of cannibals was a member of Father Huc's congregation.

1852. Like that of his superior and companion, his Chinese experience thus lasted some eleven years.

After his return to France, the publication of his first book won him fame and a certain amount of lionization that seems to have slightly gone to his head. Besides, it obviously must not have been easy for him to readjust to conventual life; for a man who had just been riding on the highways of Central Asia, sharing the free life of proud nomads, and who was used to sleeping by campfires under the stars, petty routine and discipline probably became very difficult to bear. Huc wrote to the superior-general of his congregation, "Community life is incompatible with my temperament," and offered his resignation, which was accepted in December 1853. Pelliot, who seems to have been able to consult Lazarist archives on this matter, added: "The true reason for his leaving the Lazarists is of a more delicate nature. Huc, like Gabet, had taken certain liberties with his priestly vows during his travels, and afterwards carried on in similar fashion." This comment is remarkable more for its understatement than for its clarity. Later, the French Ministry of Religious Affairs suggested twice that Huc be made a bishop, but, as Pelliot said, each time "Church authorities opposed the move, not on doctrinal grounds, but for reasons of personal conduct."

Like Gabet, Huc's health had been severely impaired by his travels. He died in 1860 at the relatively early age of forty-seven.

THE MISSIONARIES CONFRONT CHINA

Christians have progressively forgotten that the entire missionary endeavor was originally a challenge to civilization, a provocation against the tide of modernity. When Saint Peter first entered

Rome to preach the Gospel, he was a barely literate proletarian trying to take by storm the most sophisticated metropolis of the Western world. Imagine today a poor migrant from Bangladesh who would attempt to convert London to some exotic cult, or a Puerto Rican vagrant trying to bring spiritual renewal to New York. As late as the sixteenth century, a missionary such as Francis Xavier still retained this sublime naïveté when he entered prosperous India and refined Japan as a sort of lunatic tramp equipped only with saintliness and a dirtiness that amazed even fakirs. Later, however, as a result of Western political and military predominance, things went off track, and eventually, when the diffusion of Christianity became directly linked with colonial expansion, the missionary enterprise was temporarily doomed. A nadir was reached in the nineteenth century; after the first China Expedition (1858), Baron Gros could send to Napoléon III this typical telegram: "China is now being opened at last to Christianity, the true source of all civilization, as well as to the commerce and industry of Western nations."

In such a perspective, the ideal target of all missionary activity is still provided by cannibal tribes. Any nation that can simultaneously be both pagan and civilized has to be a self-contradiction, an intolerable and inconceivable phenomenon, since the mere fact of its existence would challenge the Western pretension to colonize in the name of the Gospel.

The very existence of China presented this infuriating problem to the West—a problem whose magnitude and seriousness were equaled only by the problem that the West itself presented to China. These two worlds were similar stumbling blocks for each other; the obstacle was too huge to be removed, ignored, or absorbed; each was a living negation of the image that the other had made of itself; each questioned the concept of a universal vocation that sustained the other's culture: "If the other exists, I am no more universal; without universality, I cease to be." A menace that weighs upon the identity or the spiritual integrity of a civilization is far more terrifying than a menace that merely endangers its material expansion, or even its physical survival. Even when Japan was able to challenge the power of the West militarily, it worried only politicians and soldiers; it never disturbed theologians or philosophers, as it was itself proclaiming that it was marginal, eccentric, and insular. Conversely, even when in a most peaceful and defenseless state, "China throws obscurity" (as Pascal once observed); she cast her huge shadow across the "civilizing mission" of the West.

As storm troopers in the vanguard of the Western invasion, missionaries were the first to face this obstacle. They dealt with it in various ways. One response was illustrated by Reverend Arthur Smith and his notorious *Chinese Characteristics*, a compilation of all Chinese vices, which concluded:

What the Chinese lack is not intellectual ability. . . . What they do lack is Character and Conscience. Chinese society resembles some of the scenery in China. At a little distance, it appears fair and attractive. Upon a nearer approach, however, there is invariably much that is shabby and repulsive, and the air is full of odors that are not fragrant. . . . China must be civilized. . . . To attempt to reform China without some force from without is like trying to build a ship in the sea. . . . "Rotten wood cannot be carved"; it must be wholly cut away, and new material grafted on the old stock. China can never be reformed from within. . . . How is it that with the object lessons of Hong Kong, of Shanghai and other treaty ports before them, the Chinese do not introduce "model settlements" into the native cities of China? Because, in the present condition of China, the adoption of such models by Chinese is an absolute moral impossibility. British character and conscience have been more than a thousand years in attaining their present development . . . the forces which have developed character and conscience in the Anglo-Saxon race are as definite and certain as facts of history. These forces came with Christianity, and they grew with Christianity. In proportion as Christianity roots itself in the popular heart, these products flourish, and not otherwise. . . . In order to reform China, the springs of character must be reached and purified, conscience must be practically enthroned. . . . What China needs is righteousness, and in order to attain it, it is absolutely necessary that she have a knowledge of God and a new conception of man, as well as of the relation of man to God. . . . The manifold needs of China we find, then, to be a single Christian civilization.

The reader should not believe that I am wasting his time by quoting at such length these raving lucubrations. Smith's book was reprinted several times at the beginning of the twentieth century and actually achieved considerable authority. It is a typical reflection of the prevalent mentality of its time. Furthermore, it exerted a certain influence in China itself; there, paradoxically, progressive minds took it seriously. Lu Xun read it with great interest; revolutionary intellectuals believed that the most urgent and fundamental task was to transform the "national character" (*minzu xing*) of the Chinese by purging them of their collective vices. As these intellectuals were trying to demonstrate that Chinese traditional society was utterly hateful, horrible, and barbaric, they found a fresh supply of ammunition in Smith's dark catalogue.

At the opposite end, and in complete contrast with Smith, we find a personality such as Richard Wilhelm, a missionary turned sinologist, who, instead of converting China to Western values, eventually devoted his whole life to the transmission of Chinese wisdom to the West. The secret of Wilhelm's exceptional ability to perceive and appreciate Chinese culture can be summarized in a famous utterance he expressed at the end of his life: "My greatest consolation is that, as a missionary, I never converted one Chinese."

Between these two extremes, it seems that Huc would naturally incline toward the terrible Reverend Smith; most interestingly, however, he is also capable of frequent waverings in the opposite direction. The particular value of his testimony results precisely from the fact that he is not a systematic thinker; he possesses genuine intellectual integrity and has no taste for abstractions. His perceptions are essentially visual and intuitive. He grasps every issue by its concrete aspects. He seems to adopt most of the prejudices that naturally pertain to his time and to his condition, but he does not give them much thought, and can immediately invalidate them with shrewd observations directly drawn from life. He is full of contradictions that he does not try to hide or solve; and it is this very incoherence that ensures the vividness and persuasive strength of this narrative. If one had to characterize his attitude in one phrase, one could describe it as a form of sinophobia tempered with perplexity.

He is always most happy and comfortable when in the company of Manchus, Mongols, and Tibetans; these, at least, can impersonate more convincingly the role of "savages," into which a colonial missionary needs to cast his pagan interlocutors:

These good Tibetans . . . our dear Tibetans . . . among the different travelers, it was always easy for us to distinguish a strong and energetic Tibetan barbarian from the civilized Chinese with their pallid and cunning faces. . . . We always found more lofty and noble feelings among Manchus than among Chinese; Manchus were always more generous and less treacherous. . . . [Meeting a young Mongol in a group of Chinese officers:] We do not know whether our old predilection for Mongols was influencing our judgment, yet it seemed to us that this child of the desert had something that put him above the Chinese. . . . We saw him several times; we found his company most delightful. He never showed any contempt for foreign countries, unlike the Chinese, who always pretend to despise all things foreign, and more specially all things European. He, on the contrary, would listen with interest, nay, with frank and sincere admiration, to all we could tell him about Western nations.

For our missionary, obviously, the society of a savage was comforting, whereas civilized company could be disquieting: the former, because of his very deprivation, could be easily impressed ("He . . . would listen with interest, nay, with frank and sincere admiration, to all we could tell him about Western nations"); he was thankful to whoever would show him solicitude; without any resources of his own that could withstand comparison with the glittering wares of the foreign con man, he was free of the infuriating Chinese skepticism that "always pretends to despise all things foreign, and more specially all things European."

Among golden-hearted barbarians, a missionary could find a reassuring confirmation of his own superiority; conversely, the self-centered splendor of a majestic Chinese order that had no need for his services was deeply unsettling.

Faced with this "civilization that does not resemble Europe and yet is nevertheless totally self-sufficient" with its "immense population, abundant and diverse resources, superb countryside, comfortable—though bizarre—housing," Huc is frankly flummoxed. That a world which entirely ignores us can still achieve such a magnificent harmony is more than shocking. A first spontaneous defense against this unacceptable phenomenon is simply to expel it from the realm of rationality; its very oddness should relegate it to the margin of the common human condition. The Chinese experiment is so unique, bizarre, and exceptional that it cannot really concern us. Huc constantly uses phrases that underline the Chinese singularity: "the extraordinary Chinese habits"; "this odd country"; "the amazing Chinese"; "this very strange and utterly singular nation." Chinese medicine is "mostly remarkable for the utter bizarreness of its methods." Chinese music presents "symphonies that are very sweet but also extremely bizarre." In a Chinese garden, he "admire[s] to no end all the eccentricities that the bizarre and fecund imagination of the Chinese can conceive." Chinese writing "is so strange that it shocks the sight." Chinese language is characterized by "its eccentricity," and it is probably there, he thinks, that "one should seek an explanation for the bizarre way of life of this nation."

When developed on such a scale, eccentricity turns into un-reality: China is a fiction, it is an empire of lies. "The lying Chinese" is another leitmotiv of the missionary and colonial lit-erature of the nineteenth century. Huc makes constant use of it: "This speech was perfectly Chinese, which means that it was made of lies from beginning to end. . . . We knew that we were dealing with Chinese, which means with people whose sincerity should always be doubted. . . . The Chinese have developed so thoroughly their methods of lie and deception that it is very dif-ficult to believe them even when they tell the truth."

This fundamental aspect of the "Chinese character" can be identified even in the smallest and most innocent habits of every-day life; for instance, in the Chinese fondness for eating melon seeds: "We always thought that the Chinese spontaneous addic-tion to all things artificial and deceptive was at the root of their frantic fondness for melon seeds; indeed, in the whole world one could not think of a food that would be more deceptive, or of a more unreal aliment."

From permanent, manifold, and ubiquitous lies to inhumanity there is not a long way to go: "In their tears as in their speech, the Chinese pretend and deceive most of the time. Sincerity and cordiality are seldom found among them." Hence the Chinese must be insensitive to all basic affections, feelings, and emotions of our species. Huc, having observed that in China there is no postal service organized by the government, adds: "The Chinese do not suffer at all from this state of affairs; as they are completely devoid of affections, they do not feel the slightest need to cor-respond with their relatives and friends."

On this particular point, it should be noted that Huc's lunacy was strengthened by his ignorance of Chinese literary culture (he spoke fluent Chinese, but his reading ability was rudimentary; all of his literary quotations are borrowed from secondary sources). Once set on this track, his ebullient imagination takes flight and produces a bewildering observation that the most elementary acquaintance with Chinese literature could have refuted immediately: "They do not feel the slightest need to correspond with their relatives and friends. Since they look at life only from a practical and materialistic point of view, they do not have the faintest idea of the sweetness that two loving hearts can experience when they exchange happinesses and sorrows through intimate letters. They do not know the keen excitement that overcomes us at the mere sight of a familiar handwriting, their hands never shake with emotion when breaking open a letter."

Even the virtues of the Chinese cannot be put to their credit; thus, the serenity they display when dying is merely one more evidence of their insensitivity: "We believe that their peaceful countenance in the face of death reflects essentially a languid and lymphatic disposition, as well as a total lack of feeling and of religious emotion." With such an attitude, it is quite logical that he should express surprise when encountering simple humanity in a Chinese: "His face expressed much simplicity and good nature, which is rarely found on Chinese features."

The only energy that usually motivates these seemingly soulless creatures is a frenzied and inexhaustible appetite for lucre and loot. For instance, he describes one member of his escort as being a tolerable fellow "as long as he was allowed to act Chinese, i.e., to grab pennies here and there." Furthermore: "The Chinese are so deeply mired in material interests, in sensual objects, that their entire lives amount to nothing more than one long materialistic pursuit. Money is their only aim and obsession. An unquenchable thirst for making profits, big or small, absorbs all their talents and all their energies. The only objective that can command their undivided attention is wealth and the enjoyment of material things."

The deep reason for such a state of affairs was, of course, the fact that, being pagans, the Chinese were prey to all forms of depravity. Having described various atrocities that some bandits had perpetrated, Huc adds this comment: "These details, however horrible, did not surprise us; our long stay among the Chinese had taught us to what extent evil instincts could develop in them. . . . In a country such as China, there are no religious principles that can suppress evil instincts. . . . These materialistic populations live without God, without religion, and thus also without moral conscience. . . . This deplorable country . . . these wretched regions . . . benighted nation, whose spirit has never been genuinely touched by Christian truths. . . ."

As their efforts met with very little success, missionaries felt increasingly frustrated; these frustrations in turn made them see China in the dark colors of a land of exile: "We are stranded on the extreme confines of the earth, in an inhospitable land, or, to put it in one word, we are in China." Besides, their circumstances were such that they could see only the least attractive side of Chinese society. The nature of their activity not only prevented them from gaining access to the best of Chinese life and culture, but also condemned them to remain in isolation, often surrounded by what was truly the scum of the populace. Without being always aware of this situation (even though it was largely of their own making), they were constantly cheated and manipulated by "professional Christians"—parasites, adventurers, and swindlers—the rabble and the riffraff would flock and stick to them like iron filings on a magnet, repelling all decent people. Richard Wilhelm clearly analyzed this situation, which he had been able to observe firsthand, since he too belonged to that trade (so to speak):

It is evident that if a man with a limited field of vision comes to a country like China and begins by challenging the whole of its culture with its thousands of years of tradition, stigmatizing it as the work of the devil, even though he has the best intentions in the world, he will not find support among the upper intellectual strata. In consequence, the first men who attached themselves to the missions were the people who were the outcasts. The mission offered financial advantages—it provided free board and education for its pupils, and the parents were often paid an indemnity if they sent their children to the missionary institutions. Proselytes can be made everywhere by such a method! Little girls who had been deserted by degenerate parents were bought; foundling homes were instituted in which young girls were fed, clothed, educated, and married, and these institutions were soon used by poor parents as the best method of providing for their girls. Teachers, often of very doubtful quality, found occupation, even though poorly paid, as preachers and evangelists. These "teachers" received sometimes less pay than a cook or a nursery maid. In addition, the missions—frequently with the best intentions—interfered in the legal proceedings in which their converts were involved, who often succeeded in representing as persecution of Christians what were in reality attempts at blackmail on their part. The missionary, ignorant of the facts, used his position as a foreigner, behind whom stood the power of the foreign gunboats, to induce the local magistrates to give judgment in favor of the Christian party against their better knowledge. Such a state of affairs attracted the doubtful elements of the population.*

In such conditions, the experience undergone by the missionaries in the area of human relations was not likely to give them a very favorable impression of the Chinese. They remained outside the mainstream of social life; not only were they practically without contact with the educated elite, but it was even difficult for them to have normal exchanges with the majority of ordinary, decent people. In the case of Huc, for instance, mere fluency in the spoken language would not have secured him acceptance into cultured circles. There he was—functionally illiterate, deaf to

* R. Wilhelm, *The Soul of China* (London: Jonathan Cape, 1928), 226–27.

music, blind to painting and calligraphy* and still entertaining the preposterous pretension that he was bringing to China the complement of civilization that it was allegedly lacking! Such naïveté would have made him appear as a complete crank—colorful, perhaps, yet definitely untouchable. (When we remember how the Jesuits succeeded until the seventeenth century in establishing most fruitful relations with the Chinese intellectual elite, we can better measure the sorry decadence to which the missionary enterprise had fallen.)

It was only at the very end of his stay in China that Huc began to suspect the existence of a world that until then had entirely escaped him:

As we were living in our missions, most of the time we were only in touch with the lower classes; in the countryside, we only met peasants, and in the cities, artisans. This is because, in China like everywhere else, Christianity first takes root among humble ordinary people.† Now we were glad to have at least an occasion to meet the aristocracy of this strange nation. Educated Chinese can be really charming, and their company is not devoid of attraction. Their politeness is not tiresome or boring, like some people imagine; actually it is exquisite and full of spontaneity. . . . Their conversation can be very witty. . . .

---

* For instance, he could write with naïve sincerity: "Chinese writing is unpleasant at first sight, and shocks by its oddity." He does eventually add that after some time one gets used to it, and that finally one may find it to be "quite beautiful, and even elegant"—nevertheless, his first reaction was revealing.

† On this point, Huc was mistaken. With the Jesuits, Christianity had first taken root among the ruling elite, and even at the Imperial Court. On the question of establishing the Church among the "lower classes," it is a pity that Huc does not give more thought to the phenomenon. It would have been great and beautiful indeed if, out of a sense of fidelity to Christ, missionaries would have first attempted to convert peasants and workers, and if they had been willing to become poor among the poor. Actually, the problem was precisely that they were *rich* among the poor. If they chose to preach first to the destitute, too often, it seems, it was because these could be bought more easily.

PREJUDICES AND LUCIDITY

The above quotations give some idea of Huc's prejudices toward China and the Chinese. It would be a mistake, however, to believe that his attitude was made merely of such prejudices.

On the contrary, as soon as he resumes his direct observations, he immediately refers with relish to personal experiences that question or flatly refute these preconceived ideas. He energetically opposes all those who wish "to judge the Chinese according to images painted on screens and fans, and who see them merely as more or less civilized *magots.*" Because he refuses to hide or resolve his own contradictions, he eventually succeeds, thanks to these very inconsistencies, in suggesting the living complexity of a reality that he manages to paint vividly even if he does not always understand it.

A good example of Huc's attitude can be found in the way in which he resolutely eschews any exploitation of the two themes systematically cultivated by China's critics: foot-binding and infanticide. The former issue is swiftly dispatched: "Do Europeans have any right to attack the Chinese so sharply on such a delicate matter? What would Chinese ladies say if, one day, one was to tell them that the secret of beauty is not in having the tiniest feet, but in having the slenderest waist, and that, instead of displaying goat-feet, they should strive for wasp-waists?" On the problem of infanticide, which he discusses at great length, the amazing twists and turns of his analysis actually provide further evidence of his rigorous intellectual honesty; he repeatedly refers to data drawn from personal experience, which precisely confirm or amend his own theoretical prejudices. It is worth retracing here all the zigzags of one oddly contradictory passage, as it is quite typical of his general approach. It illustrates Huc's fundamental paradox: how to combine a prejudiced mind with a candid eye. To some extent it is this relative incoherence that lends value and credibility to his testimony, since absolute consistency can never be achieved without tampering with facts.

He first exposes the basic elements of the question:

In our view, it is poverty that explains the monstrosities that are so often encountered in China and that are being so zealously relieved by the inexhaustible charity of Christians from Europe, and more especially from France: I mean infanticide. In recent years, this sorry and deplorable issue has become the object of a fierce debate. On the one hand, some people attempted to deny the reality of these infanticides; such a position was absurd and foolish. On the other hand, some other people went too far, which is the ordinary result of these hot polemics where no one knows how to stop at the quiet and unalterable point of truth. Much of the information that came from China only muddled the issue. To our mind, some facts have been unduly generalized. Thus, we must now try to distinguish what is true and what is false in the barbaric and criminal practice of which the Chinese nation is being accused.

He quotes a report by a missionary bishop; the conclusion of this gruesome document should be sufficient to suggest its general style and import: "Oh, these pagans, true children of the devil, who, imitating their father, get drunk or murder! When will their hearts become moved at last by the charity of Jesus Christ?"

He quickly reduces the impact of the report by pointing out that it is guilty of careless generalization: "It is quite likely that these facts were exceptional and that, luckily, they are seldom repeated. In our own experience, during our stay and our travels in China, we have never come across such practices. . . . One is too easily tempted to lend to three hundred million people what actually belongs to one single individual, or to consider that the entire Empire should be accomplice and accessory to what happens in one single village. Hence, certainly, a great many European prejudices were formed concerning the Chinese nation."

And yet: "It is a fact that there are many infanticides in China."

However: "Should we conclude that the Chinese are barbaric, ferocious, deaf to the voice of Nature, and that they toy with the lives of their own offspring? We do not believe it."

Still: "One can find among them, as anywhere else, perverted people who do not hesitate before any kind of atrocity. We may even say that the Chinese generally have a greater disposition to abandon themselves to all vices and to commit crimes. Should this be surprising? What influence could stop people who have no religious beliefs, and whose only principle is their own selfish advantage?"

Nevertheless: "If we consider how things are in Christian countries, we should perhaps feel that we have very little qualification to blame pagan nations for their vices."

France, after all, is no better than China. Quite pertinently, Huc quotes a description of how newly born babies were abandoned in Paris, at the time of Saint Vincent de Paul.

What should be believed of these missionary accounts in which "one reads that along roads and paths, on rivers, lakes, and canals, bodies of small children are often seen, which are being devoured by filthy beasts"?

In fact: "For more than ten years, we traveled through nearly all the provinces of the Chinese empire; to be truthful, we must confess that we have never seen the dead body of one single child."

Still, he would not go so far as to doubt the veracity of his colleagues' testimony: "Yet we fully believe that it is possible to encounter often such bodies."

He mentions that infanticide is forbidden by governmental edicts, and that the administration established foundling hospitals: "These edicts prove that infanticide is fairly prevalent in China; yet simultaneously they also testify that both government and public opinion are opposed to such crimes. Foundling hospitals are witness to the solicitude that the Chinese administration extends to these little creatures."

Yet this solicitude has limits: "We are well aware that these institutions are not of much help, and that they can hardly remedy such an enormous evil, as the mandarins and clerks who are in charge of the hospitals are busier looting their resources than looking after the welfare of the children."

However, in her concern for social welfare, China appears superior to pre-Christian Europe. Still, the problem is that her efforts, however meritorious, cannot be very efficient: "to pull men away from vice and to lead them toward the practice of virtue, practical motivations and philosophical considerations are not enough. In all the provinces of China, the administration looks after these hapless foundlings; this welfare work is beautiful and praiseworthy; and yet it remains sterile because it is not inspired by a religious idea; without Faith, it cannot become alive or fecund."

In conclusion, the natural morality of pagan China is superior to that of pagan Europe. The only superiority of the West is that it possesses Christian revelation.

China unfortunately refuses this revelation: "It is a very deplorable fact that the Chinese obstinately persist in rejecting with contempt the treasure of Faith that Europe keeps presenting them with so much zeal, generosity and perseverance." On the missionary problem, Huc unwittingly provides revealing insights.

Like Gabet, his starting point is an acknowledgement that the effort at evangelizing China resulted in failure: "There are now approximately eight hundred thousand Christians in the entire Chinese empire—a ridiculously small figure in proportion to a total population of three hundred million. Such a result should be a source for worry, if we consider that it is the fruit of several centuries of Christian preaching and of ceaseless missionary efforts. Quite naturally, one should ask what is the reason for such a distressing sterility."

He is asking the right question, but his first attempt at answering it is wide of the mark: according to him, the failure of the missions should be explained by "the cowardice of the Chinese" who dare not infringe upon the prohibitions that their government has decreed against Christianity. Yet why should the Chinese government show such hostility? Huc, without being consciously aware of it, provides the true explanation. Even though he denies there is any collusion between missionary activities and imperialist intervention, with the usual inconsistency that is his form of honesty, he repeatedly substantiates the reality of such a collusion. The Chinese government,

seeing that Christianity was brought and spreading in China by Europeans, became convinced that it was a stratagem to recruit partisans, so as to become eventually able to take over the Empire with greater ease. As the Europeans are displaying more zeal to convert the Chinese and more sympathy for the Christians, the Chinese government finds further confirmation of its fears and develops even more suspicion and distrust. The obedience and affection which the new converts show to the missionaries strengthen again these illusory fears. Of course, we know all too well that missionaries who leave their motherland and travel to the other end of the earth do not sacrifice their lives for the sake of overthrowing a Manchu dynasty. Yet the Chinese are quite convinced that religion is a mere pretext that covers a plot to invade the Empire and to overthrow the dynasty. Actually, we must acknowledge that the realities which are under their very eyes could hardly disprove such beliefs. . . . What do they see around them? Wherever the Europeans enter, they soon become the masters, and subject native populations to a rule that presents little conformity to the principles of the very religion they preach. They can see what the Spaniards do in the Philippines, the Dutchmen in Java and Sumatra, the Portuguese on

China's doorstep, and the British everywhere. They may perhaps not yet be aware of any French possessions, but they are clever enough to figure out that we too must be trying to get a foothold somewhere.

Such perception would indeed prove accurate, and Huc himself was to play an active part in the very enterprises whose existence he is denying here.

Was it really so absurd for the Chinese government to fear that Christians might become a "fifth column" under foreign control? Huc describes elsewhere, with naïve complacency, the sort of complicity that French missionaries had managed to establish with their parishioners; in these sentiments, it is difficult to determine what belonged to the Church and what belonged to France: "As we were making conversation with these Christians, we felt as if we were strangely close to France. The Chinese officials were very surprised by this spontaneous expression of intimate feelings and by these relations that seemed to go far back in time. They looked worried and disturbed, and one could see that it was difficult for them to hide their displeasure."

Huc observed correctly that the reason why Christian authorities were hindering the activities of the missionaries was not religious intolerance, but a suspicion that missionaries were agents of the Western powers. This accurate observation ought logically to have made him wish that the support which European governments were lending to the missions be less offensively spectacular. Actually, he adopted exactly the opposite attitude: he called noisily and pressingly for a policy of ruthless intervention and deplored France's refusal to support the missionaries with all her diplomatic and military resources: "We ought to have put direct pressure upon the Chinese government; the time was ripe, we could have cornered it, which would not have been very difficult, considering its crude barbarity; then we should have made

the nonnegotiable demand that all our martyrs be solemnly re-
habilitated in the whole Empire. In this way the Christian religion would have been forever glorified throughout the entire
Empire, the prestige of the Christians would have been restored
in the eyes of the public, and the lives of the missionaries would
have been made safe forever."

In fact, the missions were to serve the political interests of
France so directly that eventually the Chinese government was
not alone in its fear; imperialist competitors themselves began to
worry. A report written by a British consular agent at the end of
the nineteenth century provides clear confirmation: "From information acquired through our secret intelligence in Canton and
given me by German, English, and American missionaries who
saw not its whole bearing, I am convinced that the French,
through their missionaries, whose protection of their 'converts'
sets up an *imperium in imperio,* have paved the way for swallow-
ing both Kuangtung [Guangdong] and Kuangsi [Guangxi]
whenever it suits them to start a local rebellion or
three . . . so the French claws are spread over three provinces
(not counting Szechuen [Sichuan]) and Lord knows how much
hinterland they would claim. . . ."*

As for Huc himself, his political thinking—which was originally muddled and fairly inconsistent—seems on the whole to
have followed a sad and typical evolution: starting with the generous enthusiasm of youth, it ended up amid the ruminations and
fulminations in which men of action often indulge during their
declining years, when their ambitions have been frustrated and
they find themselves relegated to morose retirement, far removed
from the glamorous battlefields of their early years. Furthermore,
like divers who return from great depths, or astronauts reentering

---

* Letter from E. H. Frazer, British consul in Fujian, addressed to G. E. Morrison,
the (London) *Times* correspondent in Peking (14 February 1898). See Lo Hui-min,
ed., *The Correspondence of G. E. Morrison,* vol. 1 (Cambridge: Cambridge University Press, 1976), 68–69.

the atmosphere, those who have been exposed for a long period to another cultural climate can encounter serious problems of spiritual "decompression," in proportion to the degree of *depaysement* they have undergone (or to the degree of acculturation they have achieved). Actually, this phenomenon presents a pathology that still remains to be studied.* Huc's reentry does not seem to have been very smooth, if we are to judge from the shrill and manic tone of some of his later pronouncements.

At the beginning, Huc had displayed liberal leanings; he admired Lamennais, and was familiar with the thought of Fourier. In his *Souvenirs*, as Hubert Durt pointed out,

he espoused the cause of the oppressed against the oppressors. He sympathized with Mongols and Tibetans who were exploited by the Chinese; he sympathized with the Chinese people who, though possessing more freedoms than it was usually imagined, were exploited by their mandarins. As he was crossing a Tibetan region that was in a state of quasi-rebellion against China, he invoked notions of "independence and dignity" and of "legitimate hatred toward foreign oppressors," and he compared the leader of the rebels to Abd-el-Kader, who, at that time, had not yet become a popular hero in the eyes of most Frenchmen. And his *ultramontain* readers could certainly not have enjoyed passages where he described the Gospel as "a God-given Constitution where the true Human Rights are enshrined," nor would they have approved of his wish to see in Mongolia "the tree of Liberty growing by the side of the Cross."

---

* For instance, according to the disturbing analysis of C. G. Jung, who was his friend, R. Wilhelm (mentioned above) died of such a psychosomatic shock not very long after his return from China. During his long stay in the Far East, he had succeeded in shedding gradually and unconsciously many aspects of his original culture; but then, settling back in Europe, his spiritual "recapture" by the Western world provoked a deep crisis that eventually resulted in his illness and death. On this fascinating question, see C. G. Jung, *Memories, Dreams, Reflections* (New York: Vintage Books, 1965), 373–77; and "In Memory of Richard Wilhelm," appendix to R. Wilhelm, *The Secret of the Golden Flower* (New York: Harcourt, Brace & World, 1962), 138–49.

In various passages of *L'Empire chinois*, Huc still expresses
the same liberal spirit. Time and again we hear him pleading
vigorously on behalf of colored nations, and attacking their imperialist and colonial oppressors. He quotes with approval an im-
passioned page by Abel Rémusat exposing the barbarity shown
by Western governments in their treatment of non-European
countries; according to Rémusat, the so-called civilizing mission
of the West was a myth, and a mere pretext for ruthlessly exploiting and enslaving native populations. Huc concludes:
"Some may find that Rémusat's assessment is harsh, and yet,
whoever has traveled through Asia and visited European colonies
must admit that nearly everywhere the conquered races are
treated with contempt, insolence, and brutality by people who
think they themselves are civilized, and sometimes even pretend
to be Christian."

In the denunciation of Western imperialism that Huc borrows
from Rémusat, there is a quotation from the Bible that is used
with sarcastic intent, to characterize the arrogance of Western
expansionism: "Let God expand the possessions of Japhet, that
he may inhabit the tents of Sem." What is both odd and revealing
is that this same quotation appears again in Huc's third book,
where it is used repeatedly and obsessively for an opposite purpose: it is now interpreted in a literal sense, and invoked in support of the colonial expeditions of the Second Empire, as if it
were evidence of Jehovah's personal backing of these ventures.

At the end of his life, Huc, who actively pressed Napoléon III
to grab the port of Tourane in Annam, had effectively relin-
quished his earlier anticolonialism; all that remained of it was a
rabid anglophobia. Far away from the Chinese world that he had
previously explored with so much enthusiasm, observed with
such subtlety, and described so vividly, one feels as if a mixture
of paralysis and frustration were now condemning him to repeat
mechanically a few shrill and monotonous obsessions. He had
devoted the best energies of his youth to the discovery of China;

but now China became a closed world for him, and he could only curse her: "Europe has received for a long time the light from the East. Now its Providential destiny is to regenerate the Asiatic nations, whose intellectual and moral sap appears to be exhausted. . . . There is no doubt that the fate of mankind is now entirely in the hands of the European race. It is written in the Book of Genesis that Noah, prophesying the destinies of the future races, told his three sons: "Let God expand the possessions of Japhet, that he may inhabit the tents of Sem."

Thus the shrewd and lucid observer of Chinese life finally sank into a sort of lugubrious and blind monomania. There are other eminent examples of this same disease. Half a century later, Paul Claudel was to follow a similar evolution. At first, he too had been fecundated by a Chinese revelation—the very best of his poetic creation was a direct product of his powerful intuition of China's baroque genius—but then he eventually became estranged from his own experience, and he ended up painting a scarecrow-image of Asia, which he described in senile diatribes as "the empire of the Devil." On the Chinese side too, the great discoverers of the new world of Western ideas finally fell victim to a similar spiritual crisis. After having planted in China the intellectual seeds of revolution, men like Kang Youwei, Yan Fu, Liang Qichao, and others retreated in their old age into conservative positions, and some of them even adopted chauvinistic or xenophobic attitudes.* Paradoxically, they finished their careers as defenders of the same traditional world that, a few years before, they had succeeded in radically undermining. It would seem that to confront and to explore foreign civilizations is an

---

* Yan Fu, for instance, a translator of genius who had introduced to China the works of Thomas Huxley, John Stuart Mill, Herbert Spencer, and Adam Smith: "I feel that evolution of the Western races in the last three hundred years has only made them kill one another for self-interest without a sense of shame. Today when I reconsider the Way of Confucius and Mencius, I feel it is broad enough to cover the whole cosmos and to benefit all mankind. . . ."

enterprise that devours so much energy that it can hardly be sustained for a lifetime. On these cultural frontiers, the strength of the pioneers wears down fast, and those who do not have the wisdom to retire and make room for a younger generation quickly become obstacles, even for their own disciples.

When Huc's ebullient vitality and spirit of adventure were still driving him across the Chinese empire, he not only admired the various institutions of China ("the mechanisms of the Chinese government deserve to be studied carefully and without prejudice by the politicians of Europe . . . there may still be many things to admire and to learn in these old and strange institutions . . ."), but he was also able to recognize that there was still "much power and life in this nation which is larger than Europe and has been civilized for more than thirty centuries." He could foresee that "this empire with its three hundred million inhabitants, and with all the resources of its population and of its rich and fecund land" ought one day "to shake the world and to exert a great influence in the affairs of mankind." And yet, at the end of his life, the former missionary, who had by now become a frail and grumpy guest haunting European thermal spas where he vainly tried to restore his health, compromised by the daring expeditions of his lost youth, was tragically unable to grasp again a clear view of China. Thus he could only conclude: "For many centuries already, the arrogant and absurd civilization of this old Chinese empire has been trying the patience of the rest of the world. We believe that this is the end of China."

ETERNAL CHINA?

This sorry conclusion to Huc's career (which I have attempted to put back into its psychological and historical context) should not obscure the extraordinary achievements he attained earlier in his travels and in his writings. For modern readers, Huc's testimony is of exceptional interest in that it affords simultaneously a historical record of yesterday's China and a prophetic mirror of today's. *L'Empire chinois* provides both a standard by which to gauge changes and an illuminating comment on what seemingly remains immutable. As such, it constantly challenges our thinking regarding the very nature of the People's Republic: continuity or rupture? Permanence or metamorphosis?

Let us take a look, for instance, at Huc's political observations.

He notes that a main Chinese characteristic is "a feverish taste for political change." And yet, according to him, most of the time this sporadic passion is paradoxically compounded with fatalistic quietism: "Although once the Chinese have launched themselves into revolutions, they can easily abandon themselves to extremities of hatred, anger, and revenge, it is still true to say that they do not like to care about politics, or wish to become involved in government business. . . . In ordinary circumstances, when they are not under the influence of some huge revolutionary upheaval, the Chinese have little natural inclination to interfere with government matters; in this respect, they display a lovely indifference." This particular point is illustrated with an anecdote. At the time of Emperor Daoguang's death, as Huc was sitting in an inn with some middle-class people who were sipping tea, he expressed his curiosity and concern about the problem of imperial succession, but his comments failed to awake the slightest echo among the other guests:

Such indifference was beginning to irritate me, when one of these good Chinese stood up, put his hand on my shoulder in a fatherly fashion, and said with a mischievous grin: "Listen, my friend— why do you trouble your heart and strain your mind with idle worries? There are officials who look after the affairs of the state; they are paid for this purpose, let them earn their salaries. Why should we bother to do their jobs? Only a fool would want to care for politics without being paid for his labors." This advice is wise, the others said; furthermore, they pointed out that the tea was getting cold and that our pipe needed to be relit.

He eloquently and persuasively refutes the myth of Chinese despotism. He quotes Abel Rémusat: "The Emperor of China is the Son of Heaven, and all those who approach his throne must hit the ground nine times with their foreheads; and yet he cannot appoint a sub-prefect outside the lists of candidates prepared by the scholars, and should he ever neglect to fast and to confess the shortcomings of his administration on the day of a solar eclipse, there would immediately appear a hundred thousand pamphlets—legally authorized—to remind him of his duties." Furthermore, he repeatedly draws from his own personal experiences to show that "in China, political authority, contrary to what most people believe, is not despotic," and that "unlike what some people imagine, Chinese do not bend their backs under the rods of their masters."

There are two forces that prevent imperial power from becoming arbitrary: public opinion and the influence exerted by the civil service. The emperor must delegate authority: "Such an absolute power, once it is parceled out, is not so dangerous anymore; anyway, popular practices always operate as a safety brake that can stop imperial whims; should the emperor openly infringe upon the rights of his subjects, there would immediately be a general outcry. . . . The most powerful counterweight to imperial authority is provided by the social group of the scholars."

The mandarins can hold in check the caprices of the sovereign, whereas the people can appeal to the emperor when they are victims of the mandarins' abuses:

It often happens that continuous and energetic popular demonstrations can correct the bad administration of the mandarins and force the government to take public opinion into account. It would be completely wrong to think that the Chinese are tightly fettered by ruthless laws, and are living under the rod of a tyrannical authority that governs all their actions and directs all their moves. Under an absolute monarchy tempered by the influence and preponderance of the scholars, the people are enjoying much more independence than is usually imagined. One can find in China a great many freedoms that do not exist in some countries that pride themselves on having very liberal constitutions.

(Lately, some Western commentators tried to make us believe that the Maoist system was merely a natural continuation of a mythical "Chinese despotism"; actually, the monstrous excesses of this modern tyranny, which attempted to eliminate altogether intellectual life, public opinion, laws, and institutions so as to exert its terror without any check or counterweight, was practically without a historical precedent.)

Popular feelings find their main channel of expression in wall inscriptions; these spontaneous posters can reduce any local prefect, however powerful, to the pitiful condition of a mere "paper tiger":

The Chinese may show docility to those who govern them, but they still manage to express their own opinions and to let their mandarins receive the blame or praise they deserve. . . . Posters offer a broad and effective avenue to public opinion: they are being used everywhere with a degree of skill that betrays long experience. Chinese posters are lively, sarcastic, sharp, biting, full of clever witticisms; in order to criticize an administration, to warn a mandarin and let him know that the people are dissatisfied, posters are displayed in every street, and especially at the gates of the residence of the mandarin who is the target of these public attacks. People gather around the posters and read them aloud, to the accompaniment of much laughter and further caustic comments.

Huc tells how, in a certain town, the inhabitants who disliked the local prefect succeeded in forcing him to leave. (The "big-

character posters" (*dazibao*) played for a short while a similar
role in the People's Republic; yet the "Democracy Wall" did not
last long, and in recent years countless brave men have received
long prison sentences—or sometimes have even been executed—for having dared to exercise this traditional Chinese freedom.)

Huc describes at great length the various liberties that were
enjoyed by the subjects of the Chinese empire (today, for the citizens of the People's Republic, this description could be a cause
for bitter envy):

In Europe it has been written, and commonly believed, that the
Chinese were compelled to adopt the occupations of their fathers,
that the professional activity of every individual was determined
by law, that no one could leave his permanent residence and settle elsewhere without official authorization, and that, in a word,
there were endless constraints and restrictions that would revolt
free citizens of the West. We do not know how such misconceptions could have originated. . . . Regarding traveling and freedom of movement of the citizens, there is perhaps no other
country in the world where greater liberty and independence can
be found. Anyone can come and go as he pleases in the eighteen
provinces, can settle wherever he wishes and in the way he
thinks fit, without any kind of administrative procedure. Everyone has the right to roam freely from one end of the Empire to
the other, travelers are never asked any questions, and no one
needs to produce a passport to any policeman. . . . Actually, the
possibility to move freely through all the provinces is a fundamental need for these populations, who are constantly conduct-
ing all kinds of big and small businesses. The slightest obstacle
to their movements would obviously slow down the commercial
activity that is, in a sense, the very life and soul of this huge
empire. . . . There is, it is true, a law that prescribes that all
Chinese should remain within the limits of the Empire, and that
forbids them to cross the borders and to wander into foreign countries, where they could acquire bad habits and lose all the fruits
of their good education. However, the number of Chinese mi-

grants who settled in the Spanish, British, and Dutch colonies, and their massive influx into California all demonstrate that the government is not seriously enforcing this law; it is merely written in official records, together with many other regulations that are equally ignored.

Huc enumerates in great detail the various liberties that formed the fabric of the political, economic, social, and cultural life of the old empire. These liberties largely survived under the first Republic, until the 1949 "Liberation" came to suppress them all: freedom of the press; activities of political "clubs"; the role and influence of the professional storytellers, who entirely escaped governmental control; and last but not least, freedom of association. There were countless private organizations based on family, clan, or village ties for diverse purposes—mutual help, welfare, defense—and these spontaneous and popular initiatives represented the best protection of the individual against arbitrary interference from governmental authorities.

In the Maoist mythology, a basic article of faith was that "feudal" China was plunged into the darkness of illiteracy and had to await the establishment of the Communist regime before elementary education could at last become more generally spread. On this particular question, which is of considerable importance, Huc's observations (predating "Liberation" by a hundred years) are worth pondering:

In China, primary education is certainly more widespread than in any other country in the world. In the tiniest village, even if it is a mere gathering of a few farms, one will always find a teacher. He usually lives in the local temple. His upkeep is generally ensured by the income from a basic fund, or by collective offerings that the peasants present to him after each harvest. . . . With very few exceptions, the Chinese can all read and write, at least well enough to meet the needs of everyday life. Thus, workers and even peasants are able to keep a record of their daily activities in little notebooks; they can write their own mail and read almanacs, public notices, official announcements, and, quite often, even simple literary works. Primary education reaches everywhere,* even into those floating dwellings that crowd all the rivers, lakes, and canals of the Celestial Empire. In any of these little boats you will always find writing equipment, ink, brushes, an abacus, a yearbook, and a few booklets that these poor boatmen enjoy reading in their moments of leisure. . . . In every spot and corner, a Chinese can always obtain some reading matter. . . . The whole of China is like one huge library. . . . You can enter the poorest house in the most miserable village; it may be utterly bare and even lacking in the basic necessities of life, but still you will certainly find on the walls a few beautiful literary inscriptions written on strips of red paper. . . .

And Huc pursues this subject by adding a few penetrating observations on the sacred prestige that the Chinese attach to the written word.

He also expresses some general considerations, still relevant today, on the fact that China is diverse in space and time; we should always be wary of her apparent unity and so-called immobility. Chinese permanence is in fact rooted in metamorphosis; Chinese unity is but a way of managing diversity: "Among

* In contrast to these observations, the admissions recently made by the Communist authorities on the failure of their primary-education system in the countryside appear all the more striking. According to *The People's Daily* (December 14, 1979), 30 percent of China's young peasants are illiterate; furthermore, it was found that 130 million graduates from primary schools in the countryside are practically without any form of intellectual knowledge. This is the situation thirty years after "Liberation"!

On the question of literacy in traditional China, see F. Mote, "China's Past in the Study of China Today," *Journal of Asian Studies*, 32, 1–4 (1972–73): 108–12, and E. Sakakida Rawski, *Education and Popular Literacy in Ch'ing China* (Ann Arbor: University of Michigan Press, 1979). Basic literacy under the last dynasty may have reached up to 45 percent of the male population.

the eighteen provinces, one could easily observe as many differences as exist among the various states of Europe. When a Chinese travels from one province to the next, it is as if he were going abroad; he finds himself a stranger among people who have different habits, and who take notice of the oddities of his physiognomy, language, and manners. . . ." For this reason, generalizations are particularly dangerous, and Huc makes fun of the Westerners who fall into this trap; he imagines a short tale to lampoon them: A Chinese traveler who speaks only his own language lands in Europe, where he visits only Le Havre; there he depends entirely upon the good offices of a stevedore who happens to speak a few words of Chinese. Eventually the Chinese writes an entire book about his "European journey," partly under the dictation of the stevedore and partly out of his own imagination. . . .

On the subject of Chinese characteristics, he is full of lively observations; these are sometimes superficial, but always amusing and accurate:

Every Chinese is at heart both a cook and a comedian. . . . All the natives of the Celestial Empire, without exception, have a remarkable talent for the culinary arts. You need a cook? No problem—take any Chinese, and after only a few days of practice he will perform to your utter satisfaction. . . . This nation of cooks is also, as we have already noted, a people of comedians. Whoever has lived for some time among the Chinese must wonder how Europeans could ever imagine China in the shape of some vast academy filled with sages and philosophers; actually their seriousness and wisdom are, with the exception of a few official circumstances, merely found in their classical books. The Celestial Empire could be better compared to a huge fair where, in the permanent hustle and bustle of sellers, peddlers, idlers, and thieves, one encounters on every corner makeshift stages and showmen, clowns and comedians working nonstop to entertain the public.

He is also rightly struck by Chinese courtesy: "Without any exaggeration, it would be right to say that urbanity is a hallmark of the Chinese national character. A taste for decency and politeness has been cultivated in China since the highest antiquity. . . . Even in the countryside, peasants show each other a degree of consideration and kindness that is seldom found among the working classes in Europe. . . ."

The passion for gambling is another feature that caught his eye—and it is a point that deserves further analysis, as on a deeper level it reveals a whole philosophy of life.

He also noted hundreds of tiny details, none of which presents much importance in itself, but all of which remain delightfully pertinent today. They cover a wide range, from the proper fashion for drinking tea to the conventional way of making conversation with guests ("conversation must always begin with indifferent matters or trifles . . . Chinese usually sit for two hours talking about nothing, and at the very end, they explain in three seconds the actual business that motivated their visit"), not forgetting small rituals such as the presentation of hot towels to visitors.*

Sometimes he is not merely content to jot a quick sketch, and then he gives free rein to his verve, his imagination fires off, and his pen runs wild. Earlier, we saw the fantastic inferences he drew from the Chinese taste for melon seeds. No less bewildering are his variations on the theme of the place occupied by coffins in everyday life. Here again, his starting point is a perfectly ac-

---

* A good hundred years later, all three points were again to impress an illustrious country bumpkin. Khrushchev described at length in his *Memoirs* the exotic customs that he and Bulganin encountered in Peking. He complained of the strain that countless cups of tea imposed upon his bladder, but "The towel was refreshing, I have to admit." Huc found this well before Khrushchev: "At first, when we were visiting our parishioners and were offered upon our arrival a steaming hot towel, we felt rather inclined to dispense with such a ceremony. Later on, we learned to enjoy this usage."

curate observation—but he gets carried away by his own verbal
exuberance:

In the eyes of the Chinese, a coffin is simply a basic commodity
for the dead, and for the living it is a luxury item, an article of
fancy. You should see, in big cities, how smartly and elegantly
they display them in magnificent shops; they paint them, varnish
them, polish them, and make them shine, to tease the appetites
of passersby and inspire them with a fancy compulsion to buy
one. People who are wealthy, and who can afford extra money for
their little pleasures, never neglect to acquire well in advance a
coffin that suits their taste and their size. . . . In the countryside, it is not always possible to find ready-made coffins; moreover, peasants do not have luxury habits like the city-dwellers,
and they do things in simpler fashion. They ask the local carpenter to come and measure the sick customer; the carpenter
does not fail to remind the patient that the coffin needs to be a
bit bigger, for when you're dead you stretch. As soon as the dimensions and the cost have been agreed upon, timber is delivered, and workers begin to saw it in the courtyard, next to the
room of the dying man; if the latter is not always able to watch
them at work, at least he can enjoy the melancholy music of the
saw that cuts the planks, while death itself is busy cutting his
own life. . . .

On every page, one finds notations that present a vivid reality.
Macau (already then!) looks like a ghost town when compared
with the dynamism of Hong Kong; doctors run their own phar-
macy business beside their consultation rooms (this system enables them to sell to their patients the very medicines that they
just prescribed); at funerals, mourners display a marvelous ability to cry on cue; there is no privacy of the mail: "Anyone feels
free to open the mail of others; it is perfectly all right for you to
read your neighbor's letters before him, as long as you eventually
inform him of their contents. When someone is writing a letter,
if you are interested, you simply lean over his shoulder and read

what he is writing without feeling the slightest embarrass-
ment. . . ." There is no need here to provide more examples; let
the reader himself have the enjoyment of discovery.

As we have already pointed out, Huc had only an elementary
knowledge of written Chinese. For this reason he is not a reliable
guide in classical matters; however, in the experience of everyday Chinese life, he is a wonderful companion. A Russian ex-
plorer who failed in his attempt to reach Lhasa undertook—out
of spite, it seems—to question the authenticity of the journey of
the two French missionaries, and more specifically he attacked
the veracity of Huc's account. Since then, the testimonies of
other travelers who followed the original itinerary of Huc and Gabet, as well as the research conducted by several scholars, have
fully vindicated the Frenchmen's claims. More recently, examination of the Chinese imperial archives has yielded further evidence of their expulsion from Tibet. Consequently there is no
more need to reopen the debate on a false issue that has already
been settled. Yet one point should also be made: Huc is not
merely a traveler, he is a writer—which means that, in the fullest
sense of the expression, he is a man who *invents* truth. He adapts,
fabulates, enlivens, adds colors, dramatizes. In his narrative,
whenever feasible, he always uses direct speech and dialogue;
he presents second-hand information as if it were personal experience; he turns abstract notions into concrete happenings; instead of developing a theoretical discussion, he always prefers to
offer an anecdote, or to compose a whole theatrical sketch. He
does occasionally take liberties with what solicitors and accoun-
tants narrowly deem to be the truth, but he does this merely for
the sake of injecting life into his record—in the very sense of
Alexandre Dumas (of whom he reminds us often in the rhythm of
his style—perpetual *allegro con brio*), who used to say: "You
may rape History, so long as you make her pregnant."

A final observation should still be added which might present particular relevance for today's readers. The China that Huc described still appeared to some degree as a mighty well-ordered state, but it was actually on the edge of a crisis. A few years later, the turmoil of the Taiping insurrection was to shake its very foundations, nearly bringing down the Manchu dynasty, while foreign aggression and imperialist looting were to trigger a horrifying sequence of upheavals, convulsions, civil wars, and revolutions, whose unfolding process has not yet reached its full conclusion.

Huc clearly noticed the cracks that were already marring the façade of the old empire. He perceived the anti-Manchu feelings of the population ("this notion that the Manchu dynasty was finished, and that it was time for another dynasty to replace it, was already then [in 1846] quite widespread among the Chinese, and during our journey we heard it often expressed";* furthermore, he also described an anti-Manchu riot that he witnessed in a city in Hubei, at the end of a festival); he noted that the dynasty had already lost all its vitality ("since the establishment of the Manchu dynasty, everything is languishing and dying everywhere in the Empire; one does not see these huge enterprises anymore, these gigantic engineering works that are the hallmark of a healthy and powerful nation"), and that the civil-service system had become decadent and corrupt ("today, all that remains of this magnificent administrative system is merely a hollow theory; with very few exceptions, it does not exist any longer, except on paper; the mandarins are nothing but a formidable and majestic association of petty tyrants and big thieves strongly organized to oppress and rob the people"). His conclusion is dark: "The Chinese are living today in one of those eras when evil far outweighs good. Morality, the arts, industry, everything is decaying in their country; unrest and poverty are growing fast. . . ."

---

* The dynasty whose fall could already be foreseen in 1846 managed to survive until 1911! The forecast was accurate—but Chinese history has a rhythm of its own.

He was struck by the rapid impoverishment of this country, which, until the eighteenth century, was the most powerful and wealthy on earth, as well as the related and frightening problem of the population increase: "We believe that the population figure of 361 million, however astounding, is probably accurate. Faced with this, one feels crushed by a feeling of despair and wonders what kind of future is in store for such a gigantic gathering of people, which the earth cannot support anymore." Simultaneously, he was perfectly aware (as we have already noted) that China, "with the enormous potential of a dynamic population larger than Europe's, and with its three-thousand-year-old civilization," presented a magnificent capacity for "shaking the world and for exerting a greater impact upon the affairs of mankind."

Today, as we have developed more intimate relations with this nation and as we have become better acquainted with its culture, this splendid potential appears even more evident. Yet, at the same time, alas, in a China that has not fully awakened from the Maoist nightmare, and that is painstakingly groping its way out of what its leaders themselves called "ten years of fascist terror," the twofold pressure of poverty and overpopulation (if we are to believe the alarms sounded by Mao's hapless successors) have dramatically increased far beyond Huc's most pessimistic premonitions.

BIBLIOGRAPHICAL NOTE

The two best studies on Huc were written by Paul Pelliot: "Le Voyage de MM. Gabet et Huc à Lhasa" (book review of the 1924 reprint of *Souvenirs d'un voyage dans la Tartarie et le Thibet* [Paris: Gaume Frères, 1850], *Toung Pao* 24 (1926), 133–78;

and the introduction to the 1928 reprint of the Hazlitt translation of this same book (*Travels in Tartary, Thibet and China* [New York & London: Harper & Brothers, 1928]). The latter essay contains a certain amount of new information; after having written his first article, Pelliot must have had access to the Lazarist archives.

Prjevalsky's calumnies (this Russian general had expressed doubts as to the authenticity of the two missionaries' expedition) were effectively refuted by Prince Henri-Philippe d'Orléans in *Le Père Huc et ses critiques* (Paris: Calmann-Lévy, 1893). As to the later attacks by Jean Bouchot in "Les Plagiats du Père Huc," *Revue Indochinoise* (Nov.–Dec. 1924): 341–63, they were perfectly meaningless, since they did not bear upon Huc's journey, but were merely concerned with his last work, which is indeed a compilation (bordering on plagiarism) of earlier authors on China.

The incident of the expulsion of the missionaries from Lhasa was first studied by Henri Cordier in "L'Expulsion de MM. Huc et Gabet du Tibet," (*Bulletin de géographie historique et descriptive*, 1909, which was reprinted in *Mélanges d'histoire et de géographie orientales*, 1: 281–95), and again by Schuyler Camman in "New Light on Huc and Gabet: Their Expulsion from Lhasa in 1846," *Far Eastern Quarterly*, 1(1942): 348–63.

I found a rich source of information and inspiration in the manuscript (unfortunately not published) of a public lecture given in 1974 by Hubert Durt at the Institut Franco-Japonais in Kyoto, on "Le Voyage en Orient dans la littérature romantique."

On the question of Huc and Gabet's relations with the Lazarist Order (which resulted in the former's departure and the latter's expulsion), the answer to this riddle must lie in the Lazarist archives in Paris. I never had the opportunity to examine them; I only hope that one day some inquisitive scholar will be able to throw more light on this affair.

On the large and fascinating issue of the attitudes and psychological reactions of Westerners to China since the nineteenth century, Lo Hui-min, *The Tradition and Prototypes of the China Watcher* (Canberra: Australian National University, 1978), provides a short and witty introduction.

ORIENTALISM
AND SINOLOGY*

■　　　■　　　■　　　■　　　■

E dward Said's main contention is that "no production of
knowledge in the human sciences can ever ignore or dis-
claim the author's involvement as a human subject in his
own circumstances." Translated into plain English, this would
seem to mean simply that no scholar can escape his original condition: his own national, cultural, political, and social prejudices
are bound to be reflected in his work. Such a commonsense state-

* Reply to an inquiry launched by the Asian Studies Association of Australia: scholars involved in different areas of Asian studies were invited to comment on the
relevance of Edward Said's *Orientalism* (New York: Pantheon, 1979) to the problems entailed in the approaches and methods of their respective fields.

95

ment hardly warrants any debate. Actually, Said's own book is an excellent case in point; *Orientalism* could obviously have been written by no one but a Palestinian scholar with a huge chip on his shoulder and a very dim understanding of the European academic tradition (here perceived through the distorted prism of a certain type of American university, with its brutish hyperspecialization, nonhumanistic approach, and close, unhealthy links with government).*

My task here is not to write a review of *Orientalism* (thank God!), but merely to see whether Said's arguments present any relevance for Chinese studies.

Said seems to include "sinology" implicitly in his concept of "orientalism." (I insist on the word *seems*; the point remains obscure, like a great many other points in his book.) Said's contention is that whenever an orientalist makes a statement in his own specialized area, this statement accrues automatically to the broader picture of a mythical "East." I do not know whether this is true for scholars involved with Near and Middle East studies, but it certainly does not apply to sinologists. The intellectual and physical boundaries of the Chinese world are sharply defined; they encompass a reality that is so autonomous and singular that no sinologist in his right mind would ever dream of extending any sinological statement to the non-Chinese world. For a serious sinologist (or for any thinking person, for that matter) concepts such as "Asia" or "the East" never presented any useful mean-

---

* The words "European" and "American" are to be understood here as abstract categories, not as geographical notions. Actually, I wonder to what extent the European academic tradition can still be found in Europe. Quite recently, the Dean of the Asian Studies Faculty of one of the oldest and most prestigious European universities sent me a warm and generous invitation to come and lecture on Chinese classical culture. In his innocence, he added, "As our university has now established with the People's Republic of China an important exchange program, which should not be put in jeopardy, it would be best if your lectures would not touch on contemporary issues." What shocked me most was that he obviously felt this was a perfectly sensible and decent proposition.

ing. No sinologist would ever consider himself an orientalist. (Some sinologists, it is true, may occasionally be seen participating in one of those huge fairs that are periodically held under the name of "International Orientalist Congress," but this is simply because similar junkets undertaken under the mere auspices of the Club Méditerranée would not be tax deductible.)

*Orientalism is a colonialist-imperialist conspiracy:** Quite possibly. To some extent, it may also be true for sinology. Who knows? One day it will perhaps be discovered that the best studies on Tang poetry and on Song painting have all been financed by the CIA—a fact that should somehow improve the public image of this much-maligned organization.

Orientalists hate and despise the Orient; they deny its intellectual existence and try to turn it into a vacuum: Whether most sinologists love China or hate it is largely irrelevant. One important fact is absolutely evident: Western sinology in its entirety is a mere footnote appended to the huge sinological corpus that Chinese intellectuals have been building for centuries to this day. The Chinese are our first guides and teachers in the exploration of their culture and history; fools who ignore this evidence do so at their own risk and pay dearly for it. Further, it should be noted that today a significant proportion of the leading sinologists in the Western academic world *are* Chinese: through their teaching and research, they play a decisive role in Western sinology.

The notion of an "other" culture is of questionable use, as it seems to end inevitably in self-congratulation, or hostility and aggression: Why could it not equally well end in admiration, wonder-

---

* The passages in italics summarize various points made by Said (when quotation marks are used, they reproduce his own words). Some readers may rightly feel that my approach to this serious topic is selective, arbitrary, incoherent, and flippant. I could not agree more with such criticism—I merely tried to imitate Said's method.

ment, increased self-knowledge, relativization, and readjust-
ment of one's own values, awareness of the limits of one's own
civilization? Actually, most of the time, all of these seem to be
the natural outcome of our study of China (and it is also the reason why Chinese should be taught in Western countries as a fundamental discipline of the humanities at the secondary-school
level, in conjunction with, or as an alternative to, Latin and
Greek). Joseph Needham summed up neatly what is the common
feeling of most sinologists: "Chinese civilization presents the irresistible fascination of what is totally 'other,' and only what is
totally 'other' can inspire the deepest love, together with a strong
desire to know it." From the great Jesuit scholars of the sixteenth
century down to the best sinologists of today, we can see that
there was never a more powerful antidote to the temptation of
Western ethnocentrism than the study of Chinese civilization. (It
is not a coincidence that Said, in his denunciation of "illiberal
ethnocentrism," found further ammunition for his good fight, in
the writings of a *sinologist* who was attacking the naïve and arrogant statement of a French philosopher describing Thomistic
philosophy as "gathering up the whole of human tradition." Indignant rejection of such crass provincialism will always come
most spontaneously to any sinologist.)

*"Interesting work is more likely to be produced by scholars whose
allegiance is to a discipline defined intellectually and not to a field
like Orientalism, [which is] defined either canonically, imperially,
or geographically"*: The sinological field is defined linguisti-
cally; for this very reason, the concept of sinology is now being
increasingly questioned (actually, in the John King Fairbank
Center for Chinese Studies at Harvard, I have heard it recently
used as a term of abuse). Perhaps we ought to rejoice now as we
see more historians, philosophers, students of literature, legal
scholars, economists, political scientists, and others venturing
into the Chinese field, equipped with all the intellectual tools of

their original disciplines. Still, this new trend is encountering one stubborn and major obstacle that is not likely ever to disappear: no specialist, whatever his area of expertise, can expect to contribute significantly to our knowledge of China without first mastering the Chinese literary language. To be able to read classical and modern Chinese it is necessary to undergo a fairly long and demanding training that can seldom be combined with the acquisition and cultivation of another discipline. For this reason, sinology is bound to survive, in fact, if not necessarily in name, as one global, multidisciplinary, humanistic undertaking, based solely upon a specific language prerequisite. Actually, this situation, imposed by the nature of things, does have its advantages. Chinese civilization has an essentially *holistic* character that condemns all narrowly specialized approaches to grope in the dark and miss their target—as was well illustrated a few years ago by the spectacular blunders of *nearly all* the "contemporary China" specialists. (In this respect, it is ironic to note that it was precisely the so-called Concerned Asian Scholars—on whom Said set so much store in his book, as he saw in them the only chance of redemption for the orientalist establishment—that failed most scandalously in their moral responsibilities toward China and the Chinese people during the Maoist era.)

"We should question the advisability of too close a relationship between the scholar and the state": You bet we should! On this point I could not agree more with Said—yet it is hardly an original conclusion. The very concept of the "university" has rested for some seven hundred years on the absolute autonomy and freedom of all academic and scholarly activities from any interference and influence of the political authorities. It is nice to see that Said is now rediscovering such a basic notion; I only deplore that it took him three hundred pages of twisted, obscure, incoherent, ill-informed, and badly written diatribe to reach at last one sound and fundamental truism.

FIRE UNDER
THE ICE: LU XUN

> ■ Il n'y a rien de plus dangereux pour les nations comme pour
> les individus que les vessies qui se regardent comme des lan-
> ternes, et que des lanternes qui tiennent absolument à se faire
> prendre pour des messies! De même qu'à tous les surhommes
> il faut préférer ce spectacle rare entre tous: un homme juste,
> et juste un homme.
> —PAUL CLAUDEL

■   ■   ■   ■   ■

L u Xun always vehemently rejected the role of messiah that
some naïve or cunning admirers attempted to force upon
him. Whoever actually reads him—his professional devo-
tees never bother to do this, it seems—is struck at once by his
disconcerting ambiguities. In fact, he was so paradoxical and
contradictory, riddled with so many doubts, hesitations, after-
thoughts, and mental reservations, that he sometimes upset his
comrades more than his enemies. He spoke out of personal experience when he said: "When the Chinese suspect someone of
being a potential troublemaker, they always resort to one of two
methods: they crush him, or they hoist him on a pedestal."

The truth of a great writer, or, more simply, the dignity of a free man, does not accommodate itself easily to academic eulogies—not to mention the incense proffered by the Propaganda Department commissars. "When a great man has become petrified, and everyone begins to proclaim his greatness, he has already turned into a puppet," Lu Xun himself observed. We cannot say that the Communists overlooked this saying; on the contrary, they understood it all too well. The man always disturbed them; what they were looking for was precisely a puppet.

Here is not the place, however, to describe the various considerations of tactical opportunity that originally permitted the Maoist regime to select Lu Xun as the patron saint of its literature, nor is it the place to analyze the bizarre vicissitudes recently encountered by the Lu Xun "cult." We saw, over the years, warring factions fighting for the control of his politico-literary chapel, with all its relics and sacred paraphernalia, behaving like a bunch of drunken sextons who would clobber each other with their holy icons.

Actually, the phenomenon of the Lu Xun cult, with all its variations, heresies, and reforms, constitutes such a Byzantine story that if we had to deal with it here, there would be no room left to talk about Lu Xun himself.

■

A steady and monotonous flow of ritual praise seems to have finally succeeded in persuading everyone, even those who do not read his books (*especially* those who do not read his books) that Lu Xun must be the greatest, the most glorious, the bravest, the most beautiful, etc.—in short, that he is somehow the Muhammad Ali of Chinese literature. Such unanimity in the use of superlatives ought to provoke the skepticism of all decent-minded people. Let us at once reassure all the skeptics: truly, one cannot exaggerate Lu Xun's importance, even though his genuine greatness has little to do with the posthumous myth that was eventually built up by the Communists when it became for them a matter of picking up his inheritance—this fantastic capital of popularity he won for himself with his unrelenting defiance of authority and his constant sympathy for the oppressed, the rebellious, and the young.

And yet I am not sure that Lu Xun's greatness belongs primarily to literature. Indeed, if we take a closer look, his creative work appears curiously thin. Of the twenty volumes of the great standard edition of the *Complete Works*, one can omit practically half—nearly ten volumes of literary translations that no one ever reads, as they are simply unreadable. Lu Xun had a bizarre conception that the Chinese syntax was too confused and primitive to express modern thoughts; according to him, the first task was thus to "Europeanize" the language by effecting literal translations from foreign literary works—translations that would dislocate Chinese sentences and progressively force them into the mold of those foreign models. This strange enterprise reminds one of Alphonse Allais's Society for Spreading the Use of the Subjunctive Among the Laboring Classes; still, this is no laughing matter when one considers the amount of time and energy thus wasted by Lu Xun. As for his literary creation (in the narrow sense of the word), its sum total is contained in three small booklets of short stories and prose poems that would provide hardly enough material for one standard-size volume.

Lu Xun began his creative work late in life—he was nearly forty when he published his first short stories—and his inspiration dried up after a few years. To someone who asked him why he had stopped writing fiction, he simply replied, "I cannot create anymore, as I do not wish to delve further into the old world, whereas I cannot grasp the new."

His language is richly expressive and original, but also awkward and convoluted, inspiring from a famous contemporary scholar a comment that was cruel but not unfair: "From reading Lu Xun, one gains the impression that he was engaged in emulating a Japanese author trying to write Chinese." If his imagination is rather limited, his sensibility is exceptionally subtle and sharp. Leaving aside the exceptional breadth of his *Ah Q,* an immortal and sardonic incarnation of an entire nation, in his other stories Lu Xun displays all the sophistication of a tormented and rather morbid artist who remains bound within a narrow world. Pessimism, despair, death-obsession, and nihilism form the substance of this inner vision. Unlike his other writings, where he often practiced a kind of self-censorship for fear of "contaminating the youth with [his] poisons," in his literary creation he dared to give a freer rein to his private ghosts and devils. For this reason he originally gave much cause for scandal to Communist critics who, in the late 1920s, hurled abuse at him, accusing him of being "a spokesman of the bourgeoisie," "an intellectual anachronism wallowing in his own decay," "a leftover from the feudal age," "an insignificant, rotten creature in the pay of the capitalists," "an obstacle to revolution," and "a frustrated fascist."

Yet they soon had to change their tune; hunted and massacred by Chiang Kai-shek's police, they eventually rediscovered the necessity of forming a common front with all other elements of political opposition—among which Lu Xun had already distinguished himself as a lonely and much feared *franc-tireur.*

Lu Xun's political fight expressed itself in his journalistic activity. However, his journalism, which occupies the main part of the *Complete Works,* encompasses much more than mere politics. It covers a kaleidoscopic range of topics and adopts different forms: critical essays; historical, psychological, and literary observations; correspondence; aphorisms; impromptu diaries; miscellaneous notes. Strictly speaking, Lu Xun was neither a thinker nor a theoretician (sometimes his quasi-pathological susceptibility could induce him to waste considerable time and talent in rather irrelevant quarrels with obscure individuals who had given him real or imaginary offense). It would be idle to look in these disparate writings for any coherent system; all that one can find here are the whimsical twists and meanders of a restless and fascinating mind endowed with a vast culture, a devouring intellectual curiosity, originality, and independence. He had a passion for justice and a hatred for hypocrisy, a devastating satirical wit and inexhaustible resources of indignation and cold anger in the face of all forms of tyranny.

In its diversity, Lu Xun's journalism actually possesses a deep unity. There is a unity of inspiration that could truly be defined as poetical (in this sense, Mauriac's *Bloc-notes* could perhaps provide a good analogy), and there is the unity that results from the recurrence of some fundamental themes.

In a way, one could say that all of Lu Xun's writings are nothing but the pursuit of one long, relentless, obsessive, and painful inquiry into the Chinese "national characteristics." What kind of people are we, he asks with anguish, to tolerate such an amount of inhumanity in our society? In the course of this pitiless clinical examination, which often provoked the extreme uneasiness of his compatriots (in some quarters, Lu Xun was even accused of being "anti-Chinese"), he was himself, by turns, the knife and the wound.

Various other themes derive from the first one—for instance, his reflections on the nature and function of literature. For him, literature is a call, a shout that awakens people's consciousness: it is both irrepressible and powerless. Triumphant strength is always silent; only victims shout. The cat catches the mouse without a sound; it is the mouse that shrieks. Writing is an admission of failure; only losers write. By definition, the writer is a rebel; he disturbs the established order. The writer and the revolutionary have a common ground; they are both equally dissatisfied with the present state of affairs, they both refuse the status quo. They cooperate; the writer denounces institutionalized injustice, the revolutionary works at overthrowing it. Revolution is always necessary, but it also ends necessarily in failure, since its victory transforms it into a new political orthodoxy. The alliance between the writer and the revolutionary can only be temporary; their ways are bound to part as soon as the latter reaches his objective, which is to establish himself as the new authority. The former revolutionary, once in power, turns against the writer, whose activity now appears to him subversive and intolerable, since the writer remains by definition the permanent critic of all political power.

Lu Xun marries a radical pessimism of the mind with an optimism of the will. Confronted by a world of injustice, he chooses unhesitatingly the side of the victims. Yet he entertains no illusions regarding the chances of success and the eventual outcome of the revolution. Despair is probably the only rational certainty; still, the absence of hope does not justify inaction. Hope is like a path in the fields: originally there was no path, but because many people are walking by, a path progressively appears under their feet. Hence, one should start walking. The strange and haunting image of the "frozen fire," which inspired one of his prose poems, is a good metaphor for his own condition: the revolutionary fire that burns in him always remains imprisoned under the ice of his lucid mind.

One can easily imagine what an awkward fellow-traveler he was for the Communists. The Kuomintang persecutions never really harmed him personally (until four years before his death, he was still receiving fairly generous financial support from the very government he so ferociously denounced in his writings), but he felt cruelly hit when some of his dearest disciples were assassinated by the white terror.

The sight of these atrocities drove him closer to the Communist Party, which, at the time, represented for all the victims of oppression the only effective form of organized resistance. Nevertheless, even while supporting the Communist fight, he

never surrendered one iota of his critical independence, or compromised in the slightest his artistic integrity. His stubborn intellectual autonomy was soon to make him clash violently with
the commissars.

■

The last year of Lu Xun's life was occupied entirely with a bitter
war waged on two fronts: there was, on the one hand, the battle
that he openly fought against the government, and on the other,
the secret battle, even fiercer, against the "slave-drivers" with
whom the Party had surrounded him. This final conflict was only
stopped by his death. The Party hacks who persecuted him, even
during his agony (he was dying of tuberculosis), are now in Peking, in charge of the administration and management of the Lu
Xun cult.

The true greatness of Lu Xun does not reside—needless to
say—in "the love and fidelity that he always showed to the Communist Party" (as his former enemies would now have us believe), or even in his literary achievements, which, however
distinguished, have too often been grotesquely inflated.

His true greatness belongs to an intellectual and ethical order.
It resides in the sharp *lucidity* with which he faced the Chinese
tragedy (a lucidity that was also his curse, as it condemned him
to loneliness and even to the hostility of the very people he tried
to save) and in the unbending *integrity* that contained all his
painful contradictions without ever yielding to the double temptation of escape—an escape that he could have found either by
rushing into a blind sectarian commitment or by taking refuge in
a misanthropic individualism.

Lu Xun was the product of a period of transition, but he never
resigned himself to suffer passively the inhuman chaos of history.
He endeavored to interpret and to turn into consciousness the

cultural crisis of modern China. Not only around him, but also within himself, he analyzed the endless agony of an old world that still retained its deadly grip over the living, and he tried to read the signs of a new world that was struggling painfully to be born.

Having devoted so much energy to the denunciation of the evil aspects of Chinese society, Lu Xun grieved when he realized that, even after many years, his earlier indictments still remained valid: "It seems to me that the polemics aimed at the vices of an era should drop out of sight at the same time as their targets. My writings can be compared with the white corpuscles that form a scab over a wound; as long as they do not eliminate themselves of their own accord, it is a sign that the infection remains active."

We can imagine what would have been his distress, had he foreseen that his writings were to acquire even more relevance today. To read Lu Xun's works remains, alas, the most penetrating introduction to Chinese realities. Every new stage in the ordeal now experienced by the Chinese people finds at once a prophetic commentary in his writings.

A few weeks ago,* for instance, as Liu Qing's testimony reached us, revealing the horrors of the labor camps where the young Chinese democrats are being tortured, Lu Xun's observation came immediately to mind: "The most horrible thing is not a government that stages public executions, but a government that secretly disposes of its victims."

From Fu Yuehua to Wei Jingsheng, from Ren Wanding to Wang Xizhe and Liu Qing, the voices of China's conscience and hope, repeatedly gagged and always rising again in endless relay, verify the words of China's most illustrious rebel: "As long as there shall be stones, the seeds of fire will not die."

* Written in 1981.

THE MOSQUITO'S SPEECH

To Commemorate the One-Hundreth Anniversary of Lu Xun's Birth

■　　　■　　　■　　　■　　　■

People are strange. Think, for instance, of the inquisitors of old: instead of simply torturing their victims and being content with that, they had to perform the whole exercise under the image and in the name of the most innocent of all victims, tortured to death on a cross, whom they professed to worship as their Lord. Or again, look today at Ayatollah Khomeini's devout followers: it is not enough for them to butcher women and children—they must do the job in the name of God-the-Merciful.

The People's Republic of China—in the spirit of the "Four Modernizations," I suppose—does not wish to be left behind by

these glorious examples of civilization. Thus, before launching
a new purge of the intellectual and literary circles, the Communist authorities are now invoking the memory of a great writer
and intellectual; they are clamping down upon dissent in the
name of a courageous dissenter; they suppress criticism in the
name of modern China's most outspoken critic; they persecute
heresy in the name of an indomitable heretic; they preach conformity and demand submission in the name of the ultimate
rebel.

Party General Secretary Hu Yaobang celebrated the one hun-
dredth anniversary of Lu Xun's birth with a lengthy speech that
unwittingly brings to mind an observation made by Lu Xun himself: "Although bedbugs are unpleasant when they suck your
blood, at least they bite you without a word, which is quite
straightforward and frank. Mosquitoes are different. Of course,
their method of piercing the skin may be considered fairly thor-
oughgoing; but before biting, they insist on making a long
speech, which is irritating. If they are expounding all the reasons
that make it right for them to feed on human blood, that is even
more irritating. I am glad I do not know their language."

Today, Chinese intellectuals and writers are not so lucky: they
unfortunately know all too well the language of their Great
Mosquitoes. It should be noted, however, that Hu, who seems
never to have read a line of Lu Xun in his life, did not display
much rhetorical sophistication in handling this topic. Actually,
some ground for optimism may perhaps be found in this clum-
siness.

Mao Zedong was a fairly cultivated man; thus, whenever he
found himself in the mood for throwing a few intellectuals into
the frying pan, he would always first indulge in a rather elegant
harangue that would eventually become compulsory reading for
the entire population of China—whereas now Hu can only deliver an illiterate talk. Should this evolution develop further from

the semiarticulate mosquitoes of today, the next step might well take us to the more honest and straightforward bedbugs of tomorrow—good old warlords who will proceed with their business without feeling the need for so many words.

If Lu Xun was right, this should certainly be considered an improvement.

November 1981

Politics

HUMAN RIGHTS IN CHINA

> ■ How much of this is known in the free countries of the West? The information is to be found in the daily papers. We are informed about everything. We know nothing.
> —SAUL BELLOW, *To Jerusalem and Back*

■   ■   ■   ■   ■

On the question of human rights in China, an odd coalition has formed among "Old China hands" (left over from the colonial-imperialist era, starry-eyed Maoist adolescents, bright, ambitious technocrats, timid sinologists ever wary of being denied their visas for China, and even some overseas Chinese who like to partake from afar in the People's Republic's prestige without having to share any of their compatriots' sacrifices or sufferings). The basic position of this strange lobby can be summarized in two propositions: (1) Whether or not there is a human-rights problem in China remains uncertain—"we simply do not know"; and (2) even if such a problem should exist, it is none of our concern.

113

I shall attempt here to reply to the increasingly vocal and influential proponents of this theory; more simply, I shall try to remind my readers of certain commonplace and commonsense evidence that this line of thought seeks to conjure away. I do not apologize for being utterly banal; there are circumstances in which banality becomes the last refuge of decency and sanity.

The starting point of any reflection on contemporary China—especially with regard to the human-rights question—should be the obvious yet unpopular observation that the Peking regime is a totalitarian system. My contention is that totalitarianism has a quite specific meaning and that, inasmuch as it is totalitarian, Maoism presents features that are foreign to Chinese political traditions (however despotic some of these traditions might have been), while it appears remarkably similar to otherwise foreign models, such as Stalinism and Nazism. Yet "totalitarianism" has become a taboo concept among fashionable political scientists, and especially among contemporary China scholars; they generally endeavor to describe and analyze the system of the People's Republic without ever using the world "totalitarian"—no mean feat. It is akin to describing the North Pole without ever using the word "ice," or the Sahara without using the word "sand."

A convenient and generally acceptable definition of totalitarianism is provided by Leszek Kolakowski in his essay "Marxist Roots of Stalinism":

I take the word "totalitarian" in a commonly used sense, meaning a political system where all social ties have been entirely replaced by state-imposed organization and where, consequently, all groups and all individuals are supposed to act only for goals which both are the goals of the state and were defined as such by the state. In other words, an ideal totalitarian system would consist in the utter destruction of civil society, whereas the state and its organizational instruments are the only forms of social life; all kinds of human activity—economical, intellectual, political, cultural—are allowed and ordered (the distinction between what is allowed and what is ordered tending to disappear) only to the extent of being at the service of state goals (again, as defined by the state). Every individual (including the rulers themselves) is considered the property of the state.*

Kolakowski adds that this ideal conception has never been fully realized, and that perhaps an absolutely perfect totalitarian system would not be feasible; however, he sees Soviet and Chinese societies as very close to the ideal, and so was Nazi Germany: "There are forms of life which stubbornly resist the impact of the system, familial, emotional and sexual relationships among them; they were subjected strongly to all sorts of state pressure, but apparently never with full success (at least in the Soviet state; perhaps more was achieved in China)."

Lack of space prevents me from invoking a sufficient number of examples to show how well the above definition fits the Maoist reality. I shall provide only one illustration, selected from among hundreds and thousands, because this particular illustration is both typical and fully documented by one unimpeachable witness—I mean the noted writer Chen Jo-hsi, who is now free to express herself among us, and who reported it in a public lecture on the Chinese legal system, which she gave in 1978 at the University of Maryland. In 1971, when Chen was living in Nanking, she was forced with thousands of other people to attend and participate in a public accusation meeting. The accused person's crime was the defacing of a portrait of Mao Zedong; the accused had been denounced by his own daughter, a twelve-year-old child. On the basis of the child's testimony, he was convicted and sentenced to death; as was usually the case in these mass-accusation meetings, there was no right of appeal, and the sen-

* In Robert C. Tucker, ed., *Stalinism* (New York: W. W. Norton, 1977), 284–85.

tence was carried out immediately, by firing squad. The child was officially extolled as a hero; she disclaimed any relationship with the dead man and proclaimed publicly her resolution to become from then on "with her whole heart and her whole will, the good daughter of the Party."

This episode was neither exceptional nor accidental; it was a deliberate, well-planned occurrence, carefully staged in front of a large audience, in one of China's major cities. Similar "happenings" recur periodically and accompany most "mass campaigns." They have a pedagogic purpose in that they fit into a coherent policy pattern and exemplify the state's attempt to become the unique, all-encompassing organizer of all social and human relations. It should be remarked that whatever feeling of scandal a Westerner may experience when confronted with such an incident, it is still nothing compared with the revulsion, horror, and fear that it provokes among the Chinese themselves. The episode not only runs against human decency in general, but more specifically it runs against Chinese culture—a culture which, for more than 2,500 years, extolled filial piety as a cardinal virtue.

A second useful definition of totalitarianism is George Orwell's (in his postface to *Homage to Catalonia*). According to his description, the totalitarian system is one in which there is no such thing as "objective truth" or "objective science." There is only, for instance, "German science" as opposed to "Jewish science," or "proletarian truth" as opposed to "bourgeois lies": "The implied objective of this line of thought is a nightmare world in which the Leader, or some ruling clique, controls not only the future, but the past. If the Leader says of such and such an event 'It never happened'—well, it never happened. If he says that two and two are five, well, two and two are five. This prospect frightens me much more than bombs."

How does this definition square with Peking reality? Let us

glance at Maoist theory. In one of its key documents (the so-called May 16 Circular) we read precisely:

The slogan "all men are equal before the truth" is a bourgeois slogan that absolutely denies the fact that truth has class-character. The class enemy uses this slogan to protect the bourgeoisie, to oppose himself to the proletariat, to Marxism-Leninism and Mao Zedong Thought. In the struggle between the proletariat and the bourgeoisie, between Marxist truth and the lies of the bourgeois class and of all oppressive classes, if the east wind does not prevail over the west wind, the west wind will prevail over the east wind, and therefore no equality can exist between them.

In their latest book, *Le Bonheur des pierres* (Paris: Le Seuil, 1978), C. and J. Broyelle produce an interesting quotation from *Mein Kampf* and show that by merely substituting in Hitler's text the words "bourgeois" and "antihumanism" for the words "Jews" and "antisemitism" one obtains orthodox, standard "Mao Zedong Thought."*

"Two and two are five." We find countless variants of this type of proposition in the Chinese press: the downfall of the "Cultural Revolution" leaders and the rehabilitation of the "Cultural Revolution's" opponents are currently described as the supreme victory of the "Cultural Revolution"; Deng Xiaoping was in turn a

---

* Political scientists and psychologists who conducted systematic interviews with Chinese youths, former Red Guards, and so forth, were often struck by the fascinated interest and amount of knowledge shown by these young Maoists on the subject of Hitler and the Third Reich. See, for instance, M. London and Mu Yang-jen, "What are they reading in China?" in *Saturday Review*, 30 September 1978, and also M. London's review of Chen Jo-hsi's *The Execution of Mayor Yin and Other Stories from the Great Proletarian Cultural Revolution*, in *The American Spectator*, Fall 1978. More recently, a Chinese magazine for youth noted that in some groups of Communist youths, Hitler still appeared as one of the most popular historical figures (*Zhongguo Qingnian bao*, 28 September 1982).

criminal, then a hero, then again a criminal, and then again a
hero; Lin Biao was a traitor; Madame Mao was a Kuomintang
agent, and so on. Of course, none of this is new; we heard it all
more than forty years ago at the Moscow trials, and we also remember how, in Stalinist parlance, Trotsky used to be Hitler's
agent. Victor Serge, who experienced it all firsthand, analyzed
it well: the very enormity of the lie is precisely designed to numb,
paralyze, and crush all rationality and critical functioning of the
mind.

"The leader controls the past." In both *Chinese Shadows* and
Broken Images I have described the constant rewriting of history
that takes place in China (as it does in the Soviet Union) and in
particular, the predicament of the wretched curators of the History Museums, who in recent years have been successively confronted with, for instance, the disgrace, rehabilitation, re-
disgrace, and re-rehabilitation of Deng Xiaoping. These political
turnabouts can be quite bewildering for the lower cadres, whose
instructions do not always keep up with the latest shakeup of the
ruling clique. As one hapless guide put it to a foreign visitor who
was pressing him with tricky questions: "Excuse me, sir, but at
this stage it is difficult to answer; the leadership has not yet had
the time to decide what history was."

There is nothing furtive or clandestine about history rewriting;
it is done in broad daylight, and sometimes, at its most humble
level, the public itself is invited to collaborate. Thus, at one
stage of Deng's political vicissitudes, journals that had already
been printed before his latest successful somersault were sent to
subscribers together with little slips of paper expatiating on his
virtues, slips that were to be pasted by the readers themselves
over various special passages that described him as a scoundrel.

The most spectacular example of this practice will be remem-
bered by many. The day after Mao's funeral, all Chinese newspapers carried photos of the top leadership standing in a long line
in front of the crowd at the memorial ceremony. When it was the

monthlies' turn to carry the same photos, the "Gang of Four" had
meanwhile been purged. The photos, already known to the
Chinese public, were issued again, but this time the disgraced
leaders had all disappeared from the pictures, leaving awkward
gaps, like missing front teeth in an open mouth—the general effect being underlined rather than alleviated by the censor's heavy
handling of the airbrush, and by his clumsy retouching of the
background. To crown the cynicism of such blatant manipula-
tion, a little later, New China News Agency issued a report de-
nouncing Madame Mao for the way in which, in her time, she
had allegedly falsified various official photographs for political
purposes!

The incident of the missing figures in the official photographs,
though widely circulated, did not provoke any comments in the
West (with the exception of C. and J. Broyelle's remarkable
book, from which I am borrowing freely here). After all, aren't
Chinese always supposed to behave in inscrutable and strange
ways? What was not realized was the fact that however odd the
incident may have appeared in our eyes, the Chinese themselves
felt it was even more grotesque—and humiliating. The explanation for this bizarre episode did not lie in the Chinese mentality, but in totalitarian psychology.

The most masterly analysis of totalitarian psychology is certainly the one provided by Bruno Bettelheim in his book *The Informed Heart*, which was rightly hailed as "a handbook for
survival in our age." The great psychiatrist observed the phenomenon firsthand in Buchenwald, where he was interned by the
Nazis. The concentration camp is not marginal to the totalitarian
world; on the contrary, it is its purest and most perfect projection, since there the various factors of resistance to the system—
the familial, emotional, and sexual relationships mentioned by
Kolakowski—have all been removed, leaving the subject totally
exposed to the totalitarian design.

Bettelheim noted that prisoners were subjected to a "ban on

daring to notice anything. . . . But to look and observe for one-self what went on in the camp—while absolutely necessary for survival—was even more dangerous than being noticed. Often this passive compliance—not to see or not to know—was not enough; in order to survive one had to actively pretend not to observe, not to know what the SS required one not to know."*

Bettelheim gives various examples of SS behavior that presented this apparent contradiction—"you have not seen what you have seen, because we decided so" (which could apply precisely to the blatantly falsified photo of the Chinese leaders)—and he adds this psychological commentary:

To know only what those in authority allow one to know is, more or less, all the infant can do. To be able to make one's own observations and to draw pertinent conclusions from them is where independent existence begins. To forbid oneself to make observations, and take only the observations of others in their stead, is relegating to nonuse one's own powers of reasoning, and the even more basic power of perception. Not observing where it counts most, not knowing where one wants so much to know, all this is most destructive to the functioning of one's personality. . . . But if one gives up observing, reacting, and taking action, one gives up living one's own life. And this is exactly what the SS wanted to happen.†

Bettelheim describes striking instances of this personality disintegration—which again are of particular relevance for the Chinese situation. Western apologists for the Peking regime have argued that since the Chinese themselves, and particularly those who recently left China, did not show willingness to express dissent or criticism (a questionable assertion—I shall come back to this point later), we had better not try to speak for them and should simply infer from their silence that there is probably noth-

---

* Bruno Bettelheim, *The Informed Heart* (New York: Avon, 1979), 153.

† Ibid., 154–55.

ing to be said. According to Bettelheim, the camp inmates came progessively to see the world through SS eyes; they even espoused SS values:

At one time, for instance, American and English newspapers were full of stories about cruelties committed in the camps. . . . In discussing this event old prisoners insisted that foreign newspapers had no business bothering with internal German institutions and expressed their hatred of the journalists who tried to help them. When in 1938 I asked more than one hundred old political prisoners if they thought the story of the camp should be reported in foreign newspapers, many hesitated to agree that it was desirable. When asked if they would join a foreign power in a war to defeat National Socialism, only two made the unqualified statement that everyone escaping Germany ought to fight the Nazis to the best of his ability.*

Jean Pasqualini—whose book *Prisoner of Mao* is the most fundamental document on the Maoist "Gulag" and, as such, is most studiously ignored by the lobby that maintains that there is no human-rights problem in the People's Republic—notes a similar phenomenon. He confesses that after a few years in the labor camps, he came, if not exactly to love the system that was methodically destroying his personality, at least to *feel gratitude* for the patience and care with which the authorities were trying to reeducate worthless vermin like himself. Along the same lines, Orwell showed premonitory genius in the last sentence of *Nineteen Eighty-four*: when Winston Smith realizes that *he loves Big Brother*, that he has loved Big Brother all along. . . .

■

Seemingly, I have wandered away from my topic: instead of dealing with human rights, I have talked about the nature of totali-

* Ibid., 168–69.

tarianism, the falsification of the past, and the alteration of reality. In fact, all these observations are of direct relevance to our topic. We can summarize them by saying that totalitarianism is the apotheosis of *subjectivism*.* In *Nineteen Eighty-four*, the starting point of Winston Smith's revolt lies in this sudden awareness: "The party told you to reject the evidence of your eyes and ears. It was their final, most essential command." (Once more, see the falsified photos of the Chinese leadership on Tian'anmen!) "His heart sank as he thought of the enormous power arrayed against him. . . . And yet he was in the right! The obvious, the silly, and the true had got to be defended. Truisms are true, hold on to that! The solid world exists, its laws do not change. Stones are hard, water is wet, objects unsupported fall toward the earth's center. . . . If that is granted, all else follows."

Objectivism—the belief that there is an objective truth whose existence is independent of arbitrary dogma and ideology—is thus the cornerstone of intellectual freedom and human dignity, and as such, it is the main stumbling block for totalitarianism.

Objectivism, as opposed to totalitarianism, can take essentially two forms: legality or morality. For historicocultural reasons, Western civilization seems to have put more emphasis on legality, while Chinese civilization was more inclined toward morality. Yet to oppose the two concepts, as some admirers of Maoism have attempted to do,† betrays a complete misreading

---

* This point was well made by George Watson in a public lecture on "Orwell's Political Language," delivered in 1977 at the Humanities Research Center, Australian National University, Canberra. Watson, author of *Politics and Literature in Great Britain* (London: Macmillan, 1977), is Fellow of St. John's College, Cambridge University.

† They say, for instance, "Chinese authorities emphasize morality rather than legality," meaning that if the People's Republic lacks legality, it is essentially because it is more concerned with other values, such as morality. As I am trying to show here, the Maoist regime is bent on destroying morality as much as legality, and *for the same reasons*. The pathetic thing is that our Western advocates of

of both notions. In traditional China, "morality" (which meant essentially Confucianism) was the main bulwark against incipient totalitarianism. This question was best expounded by the Chinese historian Yu Ying-shih in a masterful essay ("Anti-intellectualism in Chinese Traditional Politics," *Ming Pao Monthly,* February and March 1976) which could be schematically summarized as follows: Confucianism described the world in terms of a dualism; on the one hand there is the concrete, changing realm of actual politics, on the other hand there is the realm of abstract, permanent principles. The duty of the scholar-politician is to serve the ruler insofar as the ruler's behavior and policies harmonize with the unchanging moral principles, which provide a stable reference by which to judge them. In case of a clash between the two realms, the Confucian scholar must, in the strong and unambiguous words of Xun Zi, "follow the principles and disobey the Prince."*

Maoism may even be of good faith; they sincerely believe in the existence of a Maoist *morality* because in their own callousness, they never perceive the distinction between *morality* and *moralism.* That moralistic concern can result in essentially immoral measures is most graphically illustrated by the sexual repression exerted in Maoist China: as we know, in some circumstances, homosexuals can be executed on the spot, without judgment; promiscuous women can be sentenced to a minimum of five years' hard labor, and so on. That some people here can read in such measures a concern for "morality" is what frightens me most!

* This situation was also aptly summarized by Franz Michael:

The officials could oppose government policy if they felt it to be in disagreement with their interpretation of Confucian beliefs. . . . Among the scholar-gentry at large, and, to a certain degree, among the officials, there could then be political opposition. . . . The basis of this was the fact that the fundamental loyalty was to the Confucian system itself and not to the prevailing government's policy; the gentry were the guardians and propagators of the Confucian system as such, they were not bound by an emperor's verdict on its right interpretation. . . . The gentry did not owe the emperor unconditional obedience. . . . *The significant factor in the Chinese situation was that the bureaucracy-gentry had recourse to an ideology outside the control of the emperor.*

(Quoted by F. Mote: "The Growth of Chinese Despotism," *Oriens Extremus,* 1961: 8.)

For this reason Maoist legality *and* Maoist morality are equally inconceivable; both are self-contradictions (the same applies to Stalinist or Nazi legality or morality; the terms are mutually exclusive). Mao himself readily and cynically acknowledged this situation; for his subordinates, however (as for Stalin's), in practice this created an increasingly dangerous and frightening predicament to the point where a number of old and prestigious Communist leaders could be bullied, persecuted, and even tortured to death during the "Cultural Revolution." Those who survived the turmoil, having come so close to being devoured by the very beast they themselves had raised, suddenly discovered the urgent need to establish some sort of legality. Their appeals, which filled the pages of the *People's Daily* two years after Mao's death, were pathetic, because they ran against the nature of the regime. Establishment of legality would mean the end of the system; with legal boundaries, Party authority would cease to be infallible and absolute, and a genuine rule of law would mark the end of its ideological rule. From a Communist point of view, such a situation would obviously be inconceivable.

It is in this context of quintessential—indeed, *institutional*—illegality that the human-rights question must be considered. In other words, for such a system, the very concept of human rights is necessarily meaningless. Thus, in this respect, the historical record of the regime could be characterized as a continuous and ruthless war waged by the Communist government against the Chinese people. Let us briefly enumerate here a few episodes selected at random, merely as illustrations.

■ Liquidation of counterrevolutionaries, land reform, "Three Antis" and "Five Antis" campaigns (1949–52). Five million executions (conservative estimate, advanced by one of the most cautious and respected specialists of contemporary Chinese history, Jacques Guillermaz, in *Le Parti Communiste chinois au pouvoir* [Paris: Payot, 1972], 33, *n.* 1).

■ "Anti-rightist campaign" (1957). According to the figures issued by the Minister for Public Security, during the period from
June to October alone, "100,000 counterrevolutionaries and bad
elements were unmasked and dealt with"; 1,700,000 subjected
to police investigation; several million sent to the countryside for
"reeducation."

■ "Cultural Revolution" (1966–69). No total figures are available
as yet. By Peking's own admission, the losses were heavy. In the
last interview he granted to Edgar Snow, Mao Zedong said that
foreign journalists, even in their most sensational reporting, had
grossly underestimated the actual amount of violence and blood-
shed. A full and methodical count still remains to be established
from the various figures that are already available at the local
level (90,000 victims in Sichuan province alone, 40,000 in
Guangdong). The trial of the "Gang of Four" was an opportunity
for further official disclosures on the enormous scope of these
atrocities.

■ The anti–Lin Biao and anti-Confucius campaigns (1973–75),
and then the campaign for the denunciation of the "Gang of Four"
(1976–78), were both accompanied by waves of arrests and executions. Finally, in 1979, the Democracy Walls were outlawed
and the Democracy movement was suppressed. Arbitrary arrests
and heavy sentences based on trumped-up charges eliminated
vast numbers of courageous and idealistic young people and finally destroyed all hopes for genuine political reform within the
Chinese Communist system.

Political and intellectual dissent in Communist China has produced an endless list of martyrs. The first victims fell well before
the establishment of the People's Republic, as early as the
Yan'an period. Later on, the repressions that successively followed the "Hundred Flowers" and the "Cultural Revolution" dec-
imated the intellectual and political elite of the entire country.

Besides these illustrious victims, however, we should not forget the immense crowd of humble, anonymous people who were subjected to mass arrests—as happened in the aftermath of the huge anti-Maoist demonstration in Tian'anmen Square (April 5, 1976), or who are suffering individual persecution all over China. They are imprisoned, condemned to hard labor, or even executed merely for having expressed unorthodox opinions; no one takes notice of them, they never make the headlines in our newspapers. It is only by chance encounter that sometimes, here and there, a more than usually attentive visitor comes across their names and records their fate, from ordinary public notices posted in the streets. Moreover, besides these political dissenters, countless religious believers are also branded as criminals and sent to labor camps simply because they choose to remain loyal to their church and to their faith.

The Chinese "Gulag" is a gigantic topic that has been well described by firsthand witnesses—Jean Pasqualini (Bao Ruowang) and Rudolf Chelminski, *Prisoner of Mao* (New York: Coward McCann & Geoghegan, 1973), and Lai Ying, *The Thirtysixth Way* (New York: Doubleday, 1969). The reading of these accounts is a basic duty for everyone who professes the slightest concern for China. I have commented elsewhere (in *Broken Images*) on the central relevance of the labor camps for any meaningful analysis of the nature of the Maoist regime. Suffice it to say here that whoever wishes to dispose of the human-rights issue in China without first tackling this particular subject is either irresponsible or a fraud.

Zhou Enlai observed quite accurately (in 1959) that "the present of the Soviet Union is the future of China." There will be, in the future, Chinese Solzhenitsyns to provide us with the fully documented picture of what Maoism in action actually meant for millions of individuals. Yet it should be remarked that the most amazing thing about Solzhenitsyn's impact is that the West reacted to it as if it were *news*. Actually, Solzhenitsyn's unique contribution lies in the volume and precision of his catalogue of atrocities—but basically *he revealed nothing new*. On the essential points, information about Soviet reality has been available for more than forty years, through the firsthand testimonies of unimpeachable witnesses such as Boris Souvarine, Victor Serge, Anton Ciliga, and others. Practically no one heard of it at the time because no one wanted to hear; it was inconvenient and inopportune. In the foreword to the 1977 edition of his classic essay on Stalin, originally published in 1935, Souvarine recalls the incredible difficulties he had in finding a publisher for it in the West. Everywhere the intellectual elite endeavoured to suppress the book: "It is going to needlessly harm our relations with Moscow." Only Malraux, adventurer and phony hero of the leftist intelligentsia, had the guts and cynicism to state his position clearly in a private conversation: "Souvarine, I believe that you and your friends are right. However, at this stage, do not count on me to support you. I shall be on your side only when you will be on top (*Je serai avec vous quand vous serez les plus forts*)!" How many times have we heard variants of that same phrase!

On the subject of China, how many colleagues came to express private support and sympathy (these were still the bravest!), apologizing profusely for not being able to say the same things in public: "You must understand my position . . . my professional commitments . . . I must keep my channels of communication open with the Chinese Embassy . . . I am due to go on a mission to Peking. . . ."

■

Finally, I would like to examine successively the various methods that have been adopted in the West to dodge the issue of human rights in China.

The first line of escape is the one I have just mentioned. It is to say, "We do not know for sure, we do not have sufficient information on the subject." Actually, there are enough documents, books, and witnesses to occupy entire teams of researchers for years to come. Of course, much more material is bound to surface; however, when the Chinese Solzhenitsyns begin methodically to expose the Maoist era in all its details, anyone who exclaims in horrified shock, "My God! had we only known!" will be a hypocrite and a liar. We already know the main outlines; basically there can be no new revelations, only the filling in of more details. The essential information has been available practically since the establishment of the regime, and everyone even slightly acquainted with Chinese affairs is aware of it. It is true that, compared with the Soviet Union, there may be a *relative* scarcity of documentation; this does not mean (as some people have had the temerity to assert) that the situation is relatively better in China—it means exactly the opposite. Under Stalin, what Soviet dissenter ever succeeded in meeting foreign visitors or in smuggling manuscripts to the West? The Stalin analogy is acutely relevant here, since China has always kept, and still keeps, proclaiming its unwavering fidelity to the memory of Stalin and to the principles of Stalinism. The main accusation that Peking directs against Moscow is precisely that it has partly betrayed this heritage.

The second line of escape (and possibly the most sickening one) is to say sadly, "Yes indeed, we know; there have been gross irregularities—even what you might call atrocities—committed in the past. But this is a thing of the past: it was all due to the evil influence of the 'Gang of Four.' " This new tune is now being dutifully sung by the entire choir of the fellow-travelers, the traveling salesmen of Maoism, the sycophants, and the propaganda commissars—the very people who, a few years ago, used to tell us how everything was well and wonderful in China under the enlightened rule of the same "Gang of Four." Pretending shock and indignation, they now come and tell us horrible stories—as if we did not know it all, as if they had not known it all—the very stories *we* told years ago, but at that time they used to label them "anti-China slander" and "CIA lies."

The downfall of the "Gang of Four," however momentous, was, after all, a mere episode in the power struggle within the system—it did not bring a significant modification of the system. It does not have any bearing upon the human-rights issue. Violations of human rights, political and intellectual repression, mass arrests, summary executions, persecutions of dissenters, and so on, were perpetrated for nearly twenty years before the "Gang of Four's" accession to power, and now they continue after the "Gang's" disgrace. Not only have these methods and policies not changed, but they are being carried out by the same personnel, people who were not affected by the ups and downs of the ruling clique. The terms in which criticism of the "Gang" is being expressed, and the methods by which the "Gang" is being denounced, represent a direct continuation of the language and methods of the "Gang" itself. At no stage was any *politically meaningful* criticism and analysis allowed to develop; the basic questions (From where did the "Gang" derive its power? What kind of regime is it that provides opportunities for such characters to reach supreme power? How should the system be reformed to prevent similar occurrences in the future?) cannot be raised; whenever clearsighted and courageous people dare to address these issues (Wang Xizhe, Wei Jingsheng), they are immediately gagged and disappear into the Chinese "Gulag."

Since Mao's death, the pathetic reformist efforts of the leaders have actually demonstrated that Maoism is consubstantial with the regime. What happened to the Maoists in China reminds us of the fate of the cannibals in a certain tropical republic, as described by Alexandre Vialatte: "There are no more cannibals in that country since the local authorities ate the last ones."

The third line of escape: "We admit there may be gross infringements of human rights in China. But the first of all human rights is to survive, to be free from hunger. The infringement of human rights in China is dictated by harsh national necessity."

What causal relationship is there between infringement of human rights and the ability to feed people? The relative and modest ability of the People's Republic to feed its people represents the bare minimum achievement that one could expect from *any* Chinese government that continuously enjoyed for a quarter of a century similar conditions of peace, unity, and freedom from civil war, from colonialist exploitation, and from external aggression. These privileged conditions—for which the Communist government can claim only limited credit—had been denied to China for more than a hundred years, and this factor alone should invalidate any attempt to compare the achievements of the present government with those of preceding ones. Moreover, to what extent is the People's Republic truly able now to feed its population? Deng Xiaoping bluntly acknowledged in a speech on March 18, 1978, the backwardness and basic failure of the People's Republic's economy. After nearly thirty years of Communist rule, "several hundred million people are still mobilized full time in the exclusive task of producing food. . . . We still have not really solved the grain problem . . . our industry is lagging behind by ten or twenty years. . . ."

In proportion to population, food production in the People's Republic has not yet overtaken the record of the best Kuomintang years of more than forty years ago! The economic takeoff has not yet been achieved: China is still in a marginal situation, not yet secure from potential starvation, always vulnerable to the menace of successive bad harvests or other natural catastrophes.

Further, some of the major catastrophes that have hit the People's Republic and crippled its development were entirely Mao-made and occurred only because the totalitarian nature of the regime prevented rational debate and forbade informed criticism and realistic assessment of the objective conditions. Suffice it to mention two well-known examples. The "Great Leap Forward," which Mao's private fancy imposed upon the country, resulted in widespread famine (an authoritative expert, L. Ladany, ventured the figure of *fifty million* dead from starvation during the years 1959–62). Falsified production statistics were issued by the local authorities to protect the myth of the Supreme Leader's infallibility; the hiding of the extent of the disaster prevented the early tackling of the problem and made the tragedy even worse. In the early fifties, one of China's most distinguished economists and demographers, Professor Ma Yinchu, expressed the common-sense warning that it would be necessary to control population growth, otherwise the demographic explosion would cancel the production increase. Mao, however, held to the crude and primitive peasant belief that "the more Chinese, the better." Ma was purged, all debate on this crucial issue was frozen for years, and precious time was wasted before Mao reversed his earlier conclusion (before obtaining his rehabilitation, Ma himself had to wait twenty years for Mao to die).

Such examples could easily be multiplied. In a totalitarian system, whenever common sense clashes with dogma, common sense always loses — at tremendous cost to national development and the people's livelihood. The harm caused by arbitrary decisions enforced without the moderating counterweight of debate and criticism almost certainly exceeds whatever advantage could be gained from the monolithic discipline achieved by the system. Totalitarianism, far from being a drastic remedy that could be justified in a national emergency, appears on the contrary to be an extravagant luxury that no poor country can afford with impunity.

The fourth line of escape is articulated in several variations on a basic theme: "China is different."

The first variation on this theme: "Human rights are a Western concept, and thus have no relevance in the Chinese context." The inherent logic of this line of thought, though seldom expressed with such frankness, amounts to saying: "Human rights are one of those luxuries that befit us wealthy and advanced Westerners; it is preposterous to imagine that mere natives of exotic countries could qualify for a similar privilege, or would even be interested in it." Or, more simply: "Human rights do not apply to the Chinese, because the Chinese are not really human." Since the very enunciation of this kind of position excuses one from taking the trouble to refute it, I shall merely add here one incidental remark: human rights are not a foreign notion in Chinese modern history. Nearly a century ago, the leading thinker and political reformer Kang Youwei (1858–1927) made it the cornerstone of his political philosophy. In practice, under the first Republic, a human-rights movement developed effectively as a protest against the "white terror" of the Kuomintang; the famous China League for Civil Rights was founded in 1932 and mobilized the intellectual elite of the time, with prestigious figures such as Cai Yuanpei, Song Qingling, and Lu Xun. It also had its martyrs, such as Yang Quan (assassinated in 1933). However, the history of human rights in China is, after all, an academic question. What is of burning relevance is the current situation. Foreigners who pretend that "the Chinese are not interested in human rights" are obviously blind and deaf. The Chinese were forcefully expressing this very demand on the Democracy Wall, and on this theme popular pressure became so great that even the official newspapers finally had to acknowledge its existence.

Second variation: "We must respect China's right to be different." One could draw interesting logical extensions of that principle. Had Hitler refrained from invading neighboring countries and merely contented himself with slaughtering his own Jews at home, some might have said: "Slaughtering Jews is probably a German idiosyncrasy; we must refrain from judging it and respect Germany's right to be different."

Third variation: "China has always been subjected to despotic regimes,* so there is no particular reason for us to become indignant at this one." Such reasoning is faulty twice over: first, because Chinese traditional government was far less despotic than Maoism; and second, because, had it been equally as despotic as Maoism, or even more so, this would still not provide a justification. The second point does not need to be argued (since when can past atrocities justify present ones?); let us briefly consider the first. The great ages of Chinese civilization, such as the Tang and the Northern Song, present a political sophistication and enlightenment that had no equivalent in the world until modern times. Other periods were markedly more despotic, and some (Qin, Ming) even tried to achieve a kind of totalitarianism. However, they were always severely hampered by technical obstacles (genuine totalitarianism had to wait for twentieth-century technology to become really feasible). Ming politics were ruthless and terrifying, but they were such only for the relatively small fraction of the population that was politically active, or in direct contact with government organs. In the mid-sixteenth century, Chinese officialdom consisted of some ten to fifteen thousand civil servants for a total population of about one hundred and fifty million. This tiny group of cadres was exclusively concentrated in the cities, while most of the population was living in the villages. Distance and slow communications preserved the autonomy of most countryside communities. Basically, taxation represented the only administrative interference in the life of the peasants, and simply by paying their taxes, the people were actually buying their freedom from most other governmental inter-

---

* An eminent Western ambassador in Peking has expressed this point so felicitously in a communication on this subject that I cannot resist the temptation to quote him. He spoke of the Maoist regime as "authoritarianism tempered by Marxism-Leninism," which reminded me of the well-known definition of the Byzantine empire: "despotism tempered by assassination."

ventions. The great majority of Chinese could spend an entire lifetime *without ever having come into contact with one single representative of imperial authority.* The last dynasty, which ruled China for nearly three centuries, the Qing government, however authoritarian, was far less lawless than the Maoist regime; it had a penal code that determined which officials were entitled to carry out arrests, which crimes entailed the death penalty, and so on, whereas Maoist China has been living for thirty years in a legal vacuum, which, as we have read in the official press, eventually enabled countless local tyrants to govern following their caprice, and establish their own private jails where they could randomly torture and execute their own personal enemies.

Fourth variation: "Respect for the individual is a Western characteristic"; in China (I quote from an eminent American bureaucrat) there is "an utterly natural acceptance of the age-old Confucian tradition of subordinating individual liberty to collective obligation." In other words, the Chinese dissidents who are being jailed and executed merely for having expressed heterodox opinion, the millions who, having been branded once and for all as "class enemies" (the classification is hereditary!), are reduced, they and their descendants, to a condition of being social outcasts, or are herded into labor camps. These people either, as good traditional Chinese, imbued with "the age-old Confucian tradition of subordinating individual liberty to collective obligations," are supposed to be perfectly satisfied with their fate, or, if they are not (like the 100,000 demonstrators who dared to show their anger in Peking on April 5, 1976, and all those who, two years later, gathered around the "Democracy Wall"), thereby prove that they are un-Chinese, and thus presumably unworthy of our attention!

In all these successive variations, "difference" has been the key concept. If Soviet dissidents have, on the whole, received far more sympathy in the West, is it because they are Caucasians—while the Chinese are "different"? When Maoist sympathizers use such arguments, they actually echo diehard racists of the colonial-imperialist era. At that time the "Chinese difference" was a leitmotiv among Western entrepreneurs, to justify their exploitation of the "natives": Chinese were different, even physiologically; they did not feel hunger, cold and pain as Westerners would; you could kick them, starve them, it did not matter much; only ignorant sentimentalists and innocent bleeding-hearts would worry on behalf of these swarming crowds of yellow coolies. Most of the rationalizations that are now being proposed for ignoring the human-rights issue in China are rooted in the same mentality.

Of course, there are *cultural* differences—the statement is a tautology, since "difference" is the very essence of culture. But if from there one extrapolates differences that restrict the relevance of human rights to certain nations only, this would amount to a denial of the universal character of human nature; such an attitude in turn opens the door to a line of reasoning whose nightmarish yet logical development ends in the very barbarity that this century witnessed a few decades ago, during the Nazi era.

■

The above essay, first published in 1978, was essentially based upon observation and experience of the Maoist era. To what extent can it still provide a valid reflection of today's situation? In the past, I have often expressed skepticism regarding the ability of the Communist system to modify its essential nature. I dearly wish that its political evolution may eventually prove me wrong. In this matter, however, the pessimism generally expressed by most Chinese citizens appears to have some justification: what can we expect from a regime that is now solemnly reaffirming that all its laws and institutions must remain subordinated to the supreme guidance of the "Thought of Mao Zedong"?

FOOLS WITH
INITIATIVE

A Note on President Carter's
"China Shock"*

■　　　　　■　　　　　■　　　　　■　　　　　■

T he establishment of diplomatic relations with Peking was
long overdue. It should have been done as early as 1949.
Not to have done it at that time was a mistake. Mistakes can
become a source of new obligations that should not be lightly dis-
carded. In old-fashioned ethics, when a wealthy gentleman made
a poor girl pregnant, he was at least supposed to support the
mother and child, and the prospect of a brilliant marriage with

---

* This note was written in 1979. Some of the fears it expressed did not materialize.
However, it may still present a certain relevance as a reminder of principles that
are going to be violated once more—this time in the mindless and cowardly be-
trayal by the West of the five million people of Hong Kong.

136

some heiress could not suddenly free him from his moral obligation. The American mistake, early on, of siding with Chiang Kai-shek against a majority of the Chinese people, against history and against common sense, eventually bore one entirely unexpected fruit: modern, dynamic Taiwan, with its thriving seventeen million people, who, at this stage, do not have the slightest desire to become subjects of the People's Republic and who should be guaranteed the right to pursue their own separate destiny as long as they deem fit.

The United States thus had to reconcile two contradictory demands: the demand of common sense, which was to recognize Peking, and the demand of conscience, which was to protect the people of Taiwan. This seemingly intractable contradiction was quite satisfactorily solved in practice. A triangular relationship progressively evolved between Washington, Taipei, and Peking in a way that smoothly and efficiently met the basic requirements of all three parties. The main interest of the United States—and of world peace—would have been to preserve this balance.

The "normalization" that Carter so rashly and irresponsibly improvised destroyed a precious equilibrium and introduced dangerous instability. The Soviet Union has been needlessly provoked, Peking has been foolishly emboldened, and Taipei feels cornered and pushed toward desperate and ominous decisions. An element of unpredictability has thus been injected at once on all sides. In this respect, the Chinese adventure in Vietnam, which is but a beginning, was a direct outcome of Deng Xiaoping's surrealistic American experiences: having gauged to its full measure the naïveté, malleability, and incoherence of Carter and his Asian experts, Deng felt confident enough to launch this frightful gamble, at the risk of jeopardizing his modernization plans and presenting the Soviet Union with a golden pretext for the military strike it has dreamed of launching for the last twelve years.

These alarming developments are all the more deplorable because they were perfectly avoidable. "Normalization" could have
been achieved under far safer conditions if it had been worked
out more cautiously and at a slower pace. It could even have been
postponed without any real harm. The two main purposes for
which Peking is seeking closer relations with the United States
are (1) protection against the Soviet menace, and (2) modernization of China. These two objectives, both of which deserve
American sympathy and support, were already essentially secured within the framework of the already existing de facto relations. If Peking wished to upgrade the relationship and insisted
on adorning it with full ambassadorial paraphernalia, it should
have paid the price. In particular, it should have provided guarantees about the security of Taiwan. All that Washington had to
do was sit tight and wait. Peking had no other option. It cannot
mend its fences with the Soviet Union; the Sino-Russian conflict,
deeply embedded in history and determined by permanent factors of political geography, lies beyond the reach and control of
modern statesmen. And Peking cannot cancel the modernization
drive without committing political suicide. Thus it had to accept
either a continuation of the de facto relationship, or "normalization" on American terms.

What Carter proudly announced to the nation at the end of last
year was in fact that he had given away, without any compen-
sation, this unique bargaining advantage enjoyed by the United
States. In exchange he had obtained nothing, and he seemed
very pleased with it. The reasons for this incredible *marché de
dupes* are manifold. There is the pathological psychology of a
compulsive achiever who, unable to understand the old wisdom
of Kipling's law that "most of the things in the world are achieved
by judicious leaving alone" is further driven into frantic activity
by a show-business-oriented society. "Judicious leaving alone"
achieves many things in the world, but not newspaper headlines

and TV spectaculars. The irresponsibility of Carter's political advisers and China experts also contributed. Give an academic the delusion that he may play a historic role, and you can turn any decent scholar into a public hazard. As the Russian proverb says, "to have a fool is bad, but to have a fool with initiative is worse." For all the expertise displayed in Carter's China policy, it could as well have been designed by Shirley MacLaine. One small example: from Nixon's Shanghai communiqué to Carter's "normalization" communiqué, in the Chinese language versions, the Chinese managed a decisive verbal escalation without provoking any reaction on the American side: the phrase "the United States *acknowledges* the Chinese position on Taiwan" thus became "the United States *admits* the Chinese position on Taiwan." Apparently no one was able, or bothered, to read the Chinese text!

The precise timing of Carter's China initiative has led to much speculation among independent China observers. Since it occurred at the exact moment when it could inflict the most grievous damage upon Taiwan's political life, the Chinese on Taiwan find it hard to accept the notion that this might have been purely coincidental. Taiwan is by no means a democratic country. Over the years, however, the democratic trend has grown in strength, even finding an echo within a certain fraction of the Kuomintang itself, among some younger and more enlightened members of the leadership. Though still represented by only a minority within the party, this democratic tendency, supported by a majority of the population and better attuned to the reality of modern Taiwan, had time on its side and was promised eventual victory.

A most crucial step in that direction was provided by the national elections, due for late December of last year (1978). In contrast with earlier, perfunctory elections, this time the electoral campaign was developing in a way that impressed even Taiwan's most severe critics. The political debate was free, bold, and thorough; many non-party and opposition candidates were fairly sure to win, to the utter dismay of the Kuomintang die-hards. And then, when victory was practically within the reach of so many of these champions of democracy, came Carter's announcement—a godsent opportunity for the old conservatives, who immediately decreed a state of emergency, canceled the elections, and even arrested several leading opposition personalities. Why could Carter not wait just a few more days? Was it a plot? Was it callousness? Was it ignorance? Though it is unbelievable to the Chinese, the correct explanation seems, alas, to be ignorance. Carter's China "think tank" was not aware that there was an election campaign approaching its climax in Taiwan. The U.S. government spends billions of dollars on the gathering of intelligence. And yet, unfortunately, it did not possess the information that you and I obtain every day for a few cents, simply by buying the newspaper. In a world where democracy is already on the wane, Carter thus unwittingly destroyed, with one mighty blow, this precious and fragile attempt at developing one new democracy in Asia.

Reflecting upon this singular achievement of a man who, without doubt, is lofty-minded and utterly honest, one nearly comes to regret the time when American politics was in the hands of mere crooks.

THE DEATH
OF LIN BIAO*

O ur age, which takes pride in the unprecedented scope, speed, and sophistication of its information, will probably go down in history as the Age of Credulity. This is a paradox only in appearance; actually, there is a direct relationship that logically links the eclipse of rationality to the relentless hunt for exclusive or sensational news which obsesses our society.

An Italian bishop once observed: "One *true* miracle is worth

---

* This essay had been commissioned and accepted by the American publishers of Yao Ming-le's book on the death of the Chinese leader Lin Biao, to be used as the introduction. At the last minute the publishers rejected it—allegedly, Yao Ming-le's representative had objected to its "excessively polemical" character.

two." Today we could paraphrase this saying: "One *true* piece of information is worth two." The Lin Biao affair well illustrated this point: one of the main reasons why, eleven years ago, public opinion in the West swallowed so easily the preposterous tales hastily and crudely concocted by the Chinese propaganda organs was simply that in the absence of any true information, even palpably false information will always appear as the next best thing.

■

Chen Yi, an influential member of the old Communist ruling clique, who knew what he was talking about, declared a few years before Lin Biao's mysterious downfall: "Comrade Lin Biao is a truly great man; among all of us, *he is the only one who never opposed Chairman Mao*" (author's emphasis). At that time this statement was absolutely accurate, and one would have thought that it could eventually serve as Lin's epitaph.

Lin Biao was a shadowy, frail, and colorless figure who made himself remarkable for two things: (1) an unconditional, absolute, and unwavering devotion to Mao Zedong; and (2) a military genius that has often been compared by independent scholars to Napoleon's (actually, some of his battles have become models for study in military academies).

The official slogan that emerged during the "Cultural Revolution," "Comrade Lin Biao is Chairman Mao's closest comrade-in-arms," was somewhat simplistic, yet essentially accurate. The fact is that without Lin Biao it would have been impossible for Mao ever to launch his "Cultural Revolution." To appreciate this point, one must go back to the 1959 Lushan Conference.*

---

* Not to be confused with the 1970 Lushan Conference (second plenary session of the Ninth Central Committee), which was to mark for Lin Biao the beginning of the end. It was there that Mao rebuked him publicly for the first time.

This momentous conference had been convoked as an attempt to sort out the chaos created by the catastrophic failure of Mao's "Great Leap Forward." As a result of the delirious policies of the Leap (for which Mao was solely responsible), famine was looming in the countryside—it was to claim *millions* of lives over the next three years—and the Chinese economy lay in ruins. Mao, whose leadership had until then never been challenged, found himself suddenly confronted with a mutiny in the highest levels of the party. The mutiny was led by a forceful and prestigious personality, Defense Minister Peng Dehuai, a military hero immensely popular for his honesty, outspokenness, frugal life-style, and down-to-earth common sense. On the basis of thorough investigations that he had carried out in the countryside, at the grassroots level, witnessing the distress of the hard-pressed peasants, Peng denounced Mao's "petit-bourgeois hotheadedness," megalomania, egocentrism, subjectivist idealism, and increasing isolation from reality.

As a majority of Central Committee members were gathering around Peng's banner, a third protagonist took advantage of this conflict to reap all the benefit for himself: Liu Shaoqi. Liu suggested that such an open fight would be utterly harmful to the authority of the Communist leadership. For the sake of order and national unity, it would be essential to preserve intact the prestige of Mao, at least in a symbolic fashion. Mao should thus be spared any public setback and, to this end, Peng would be formally reprimanded and demoted from his official post. For Mao, however, the price of this face-saving solution would be heavy: he would have to relinquish in fact his actual power into the hands of Liu Shaoqi (who subsequently became the head of state) and Deng Xiaoping (Secretary of the Party).

As a result of the 1959 Lushan Conference, Mao was effectively "kicked upstairs" or, as the Chinese say, "laid to rest on a sidetrack." In his largely ceremonial capacity as Chairman of the Party, he could still deliver occasional speeches and address the nation, but he talked in a complete vacuum. The actual decision-making and implementation of policies were now entirely under the control of Liu and Deng. Yet Mao did not lose everything at Lushan; he obtained the replacement of Peng Dehuai by a man of his own choice, Lin Biao. At the time, the designation of Lin Biao as new defense minister did not raise any objection among the leaders; appreciated for his military competence, this otherwise dull and shy character, utterly devoid of eloquence and charisma, was not likely to attract attention or stir controversy. Actually, Mao had, by means of this appointment, put in place the fundamental steppingstone that would eventually enable him to return to power; with Lin Biao in this key position, Mao was like a chess master who, by the early move of one inconspicuous pawn, ensures his final victory.

For Mao, the years that followed Lushan were a crossing of the desert. The repeated attempts that he made to regain his lost power were successively foiled with ease by Liu Shaoqi and Deng Xiaoping, who kept a tight hold on the everyday operations of the party. At last, in 1965, using a farfetched "cultural" pretext, proceeding via the circuitous route of Shanghai, Mao finally escaped their vigilance and managed to light the fuse that would lead to that huge explosion, the "Cultural Revolution," a year later. Liu and Deng were at first quite confident that they would be able to regain control and manipulate this potentially dangerous new movement, keeping it under their own close supervision. Indeed, in Peking, the Central Committee immediately entrusted a group of their henchmen with the entire organization and management of the "Cultural Revolution," and officially approved the group's first report of activity in February 1966. (This activity had in fact consisted essentially of neutralizing and defusing the revolutionary potential of the "Cultural Revolution"!) It was at this precise juncture that Lin Biao came on stage and completely reversed the situation in Mao's favor.

Using the troops that for the last six years he had been readying for this particular political mission, he launched a military coup that secured for the Maoist camp full and direct control of the Peking Military Region. Under their guns, the Central Committee was reconvened, and in May 1966 it dutifully denounced the very report it had just approved two months earlier! Now Mao's "Cultural Revolution" was well and truly launched. No one would be able to put the fire out before the entire Party had been blown to smithereens. The whole country would be laid waste, millions of people would die—but what would it matter? Amid all this terror, madness, blood, and devastation, Mao would find his way to victory. The ruin of China was a small price to pay if, in the end, this savage chaos could enable him to recover the power that the Central Committee had forced him to relinquish in 1959.

First the Red Guards were unleashed against Mao's political enemies, who were thus flushed out of their shelters, hunted down, lynched, and murdered. After this operation, the army stepped in to restore discipline and to replace the Party, which had been completely wrecked in the turmoil. The troops of Lin Biao brought the Red Guards back to heel (in some places they simply massacred them) and imposed a new rigid order all over China. Mao's full victory was celebrated at the Ninth Party Congress, in 1969. There was, however, one shadow on his triumph: the Congress, marking the establishment of a purified Maoist party, turned in fact into the personal apotheosis of Lin Biao. Lin was solemnly anointed as the new heir-designate. From now on, the future belonged entirely to the man whose armies were running the whole country.

■

Two years later—in September 1971—Lin Biao suddenly disappeared.

After an awkward silence, Peking produced, in bits and

pieces, an incredible story. According to this official version, Lin Biao had organized what appeared to be—from the documents released by the official propaganda organs—a grotesquely incompetent plot to assassinate Mao and seize power. He failed in his attempt; in a state of total panic, he allegedly tried to escape to the Soviet Union. On the way, due to obscure causes, his plane crashed in Mongolia. He was killed in the crash, thus meeting a just reward for his cowardice and treachery.

Needless to say, there were enough loopholes in this bizarre tale to let an entire herd of mammoths gallop through. At the time of his alleged conspiracy, Lin Biao was the most powerful man in China. Why should he plot to seize the power that he practically possessed already? His position as Mao's heir-designate had just been enshrined in the Constitution. He merely had to wait a few more years for the old man to die, and he could have enjoyed the full array of imperial paraphernalia. He could have waited in complete security, since he had supreme authority over the guns—out of the barrels of which, as Mao rightly observed, comes all political power. Even if we suppose that, in a sudden wish to advance the clock, he indeed actually conspired against Mao (whom he had served with such unfailing loyalty during his entire career), it is even harder to understand why his coup d'etat should not have succeeded.

How could his unique combination of superior tactical genius, massive military might, and unlimited political resources come to such a lamentable end, even before one single move was made or one single shot fired? How could a conspiracy masterminded by such a man, from such a vantage point, simply burst like a soap bubble, without producing the slightest commotion, without leaving the faintest scar? Even if it ended in failure, a coup really organized by Lin Biao would have rocked the entire country, if not started a civil war.

As a military commander, Lin Biao was legendary for his cold, cautious, and calculating mind; his constant rule was never to go into battle if one was not one hundred percent sure of victory. Now, for the most decisive move of his entire life, how could he have failed to draw contingency plans to deal with unexpected hitches? Several military regions were under the command of his closest followers. He could easily have turned Guangzhou into an impregnable fortress. Why should he have fled to a remote and hostile Soviet Union (which, of late, he had so forcefully opposed in public)? Why did he not try to take refuge in southern China, among his own loyal troops?

The Peking propaganda organs subsequently released various "documents" purporting to substantiate Lin Biao's crimes. First came the "571 Outline," the draft of a plan for an armed uprising. We can easily grant that Lin Biao had no moral qualms whatsoever—after all, he had been a practicing Communist all his life. But to believe that he was the author of this ludicrous document, whose intellectual level would barely fit the requirements of a Boy Scouts' game on a Sunday outing, we would have to deny him not only the intelligence with which even his enemies credited him, but also basic common sense. Later, doctored photographs of his body and his wife's, allegedly taken in the wreck of their plane, hardly improved the credibility of the official Peking version. Bodies incinerated in the crash of a jet aircraft seldom preserve such easily recognizable features; moreover, Outer Mongolia is, for all practical purposes, Soviet military territory. The border region where the plane crashed is precisely one of the sensitive areas where, for years, the Soviets have been deploying their military machine against China. For Chinese officials to go there and freely take photos would be about as likely as you or I taking an after-dinner stroll on the moon.*

---

* As I pointed out in my book *Chinese Shadows* (New York: Viking, 1977), 180, the Russians, having direct access to the site of the crash, have known all along that Lin Biao was not on the plane. Earlier in his career, Lin had undergone lengthy medical treatment in the Soviet Union; the Russians had enough medical infor-

The fumbling and awkward lies that Peking hastily proffered in the guise of an explanation merely made it more obvious that the entire case was rigged. The Lin Biao affair, as presented by the Maoist sources, was nothing but a smokescreen that ill-concealed an even more shocking and gruesome reality: *Lin Biao had been assassinated, in China, on Mao's order.*

Having outlived his usefulness, Lin had become too successful and powerful for the Chairman's taste. This assassination, coming a few years after the equally ruthless elimination of Mao's previous heir-designate, Liu Shaoqi, was merely fulfilling a set pattern: Mao had used the Red Guards to destroy Liu, and then had used Lin Biao to destroy the Red Guards; now, with the smooth and efficient assistance of Zhou Enlai, he had dispatched Lin Biao. As for Zhou Enlai himself, a similar fate was prepared for him a few years later. It did not reach full completion only because Zhou was lucky enough to have a cancer that eventually developed faster than the Chairman's schemes.

The assassination of Lin Biao threw his son—a useless playboy—into a panic; with a few of his own cronies, he attempted to fly away from China (he was himself an air force officer) and crashed in Mongolia. Earlier, it is quite possible that the son might have drafted the absurd and puerile "571 Outline." He was reckless and harebrained enough to have conceived such a project. As it was imperative for Mao's prestige that his latest crime be kept secret, the propaganda organs simply ascribed to Lin the absurd cogitations and unsuccessful escape of his son. In practice, this substitution trick proved to be of limited use. For the Chinese public, it made little difference whether Chair-

---

mation to identify his body with certainty, had he been among the passengers on the wrecked Trident. At the time they made no secret of this fact, but neither did they give it special publicity, not knowing which version of the episode would best serve their own interests.

man Mao had successfully murdered Vice-Chairman Lin, or whether Vice-Chairman Lin had unsuccessfully tried to murder Chairman Mao. Whatever little moral credit and prestige the Chinese Communist Party had managed to salvage from the successive crises of the last quarter of a century, and especially after the murderous madness of the "Cultural Revolution," was, finally, unable to survive this last blow.

■

The manuscript of *The Conspiracy and Death of Lin Biao,* by Yao Ming-le (New York: Alfred A. Knopf, 1983), landed on my desk two weeks ago. I do not know its author. The publishers could only tell me that he is a Chinese whom they have good reason to trust. He had access to exclusive, secret information, and needs to retain complete anonymity.

Not knowing the author, and not being able to check his sources, I can, of course, draw no conclusions regarding the historical accuracy of his narrative. Moreover, I do not know what the author's motivations are. Is he merely trying to serve the historical truth? What other interests may be furthered by this publication? Is it a pure coincidence that this manuscript—which exposes the deviousness of Mao and shows that Lin's conspiracy presented at least an element of self-defense—reached Western publishers *precisely* at the time when, in Peking, the leading military personalities who had been condemned to heavy sentences for their participation in the Lin Biao conspiracy were suddenly released, barely one year after having been sentenced? (They were freed allegedly because of old age and ill health. No follower of the Maoist gang convicted during the same trial benefited from such leniency.) It should also be noted that the Soviet Union, which had kept quiet on this whole affair, suddenly began to leak reports a few weeks ago reminding us that, indeed, Lin

Biao was not in the Trident that had crashed in Mongolia. Who is helping whom, and for what purpose?

Keeping all these reservations and unanswered questions in mind, I read this book with fascination. Its narrative tallies with all available evidence. It confirms the basic contention of all serious China observers that Lin Biao was assassinated in China, on Mao's initiative. It provides a wealth of new elements and illuminating details. I confess I would personally question some aspects of these new revelations (I still find it difficult to believe that Lin actively conspired against Mao; if such a conspiracy ever existed, it must have been a desperate, last-minute attempt, when Lin realized that he was already cornered). But I cannot disprove them, or prove my own point.* And I must admit that, on the whole, the picture presented in Yao Ming-le's account is plausible and coherent—although all the implications it may present for Sino-Soviet relations should be received with the greatest critical caution. In particular, the contention that the armed clashes between the two countries could be ascribed merely to the private schemes of one individual seems a crude oversimplification, to say the least.

Needless to say, these pages will appear most unsettling to a great many readers. Western audiences have been particularly ill-prepared to confront the gruesome realities of the power struggle that rages permanently within the Communist ruling clique. At every turn of this ferocious fight, coups, counter-coups, purges, plots, and assassinations have been studiously ignored by our leading political analysts. "No, no!" they assure us each

---

* If Lin had really organized a conspiracy, how shall we explain the fact that after he had been killed and his conspiracy had been exposed (September 12), his co-conspirators were still active on the national stage several days later? Qiu Huizuo, for instance, made a public appearance on September 24 at Peking airport where he went, together with Zhou Enlai and Ye Jianying, to bid farewell to a Chinese economic delegation leaving for Hanoi.

time. "Chinese politics do not work this way," there are no power struggles in China, only "some policy problems on which honest revolutionaries disagree." "China experts" are fortunate indeed; the public never extends to them the elementary standards of professional competence that are normally expected from modest mechanics and plumbers. We dismiss the technicians who fail to mend our cars or our leaky bathroom faucets, but whenever the political reality belies the analyses of the "experts," we dismiss the reality.

The temptation to dismiss the reality should be particularly strong in this case, as sensitive souls may find that the light that the Lin Biao affair sheds on the nature and the workings of the Chinese Communist leadership is unbearably crude. To say that the Party leaders behave like gangsters would be a gratuitous slur on the latters' reputation. After all, even in the underworld some kind of twisted morality is still being cultivated, some principles are still respected, a certain concept of loyalty within the gang is still valued. In this respect, the Lin Biao affair will remain a landmark in the history of the Party; with it, the moral bankruptcy of the regime was totally exposed to the public, and as a result, the cynicism and political demobilization of the Chinese populace reached a point of no return.

If the sinister political milieu described in Yao's book will without doubt shock and scandalize many Westerners, for any Chinese reader these pages evoke a reality that is all too grimly familiar. The psychology, behavior, and life-style of the ruling elite are here faithfully portrayed. The sociological accuracy of this narrative is thus beyond question. But is this account true? At least it makes sense—which is more than could be said for the official Peking version of the Lin Biao affair.

October 1982

THE PATH OF AN EMPTY BOAT: ZHOU ENLAI

■　　　■　　　■　　　■　　　■

Alone among the Maoist leaders, Zhou Enlai had cosmopolitan sophistication, charm, wit, and style. He certainly was one of the greatest and most successful comedians of our century. He had a talent for telling blatant lies with angelic suavity. He was the kind of man who could stick a knife in your back and do it with such disarming grace that you would still feel compelled to thank him for the deed. He gave a human face (and a very good-looking one) to Chinese Communism. Everyone loved him. He repeatedly and literally got away with murder. No wonder politicians from all over the world unanimously worshipped him. That intellectuals should also share in this cult is more disturbing—although there are some extenuating circumstances.

Zhou was a compulsive seducer. I am of course not referring to his behavior with the ladies, which was always said to be exemplary, and anyway should not concern us. What I mean is simply that, for him, it seems no interlocutors ever appeared too small, too dim, or too irrelevant not to warrant a special effort on his part to charm them, to wow them, and to win their sympathy and support. I can state this from direct and personal experience, an experience that was shared over the years by hundreds and thousands of enraptured visitors—primary-school teachers from Zanzibar, trade unionists from Tasmania, Progressive Women from Lapland—not even the Pope had to cope with such time-consuming, bizarre, and endless processions of pilgrims. He was also the ultimate Zelig of politics, showing tolerance, urbanity, and a spirit of compromise to urbane Western liberals; eating fire and spitting hatred to suit the taste of embittered Third World leaders; displaying culture and refinement with artists, being pragmatic with pragmatists, philosophical with philosophers, and Kissingerian with Kissinger.

It should not be forgotten that besides these strange and absorbing social activities, he was also directing the entire administration of the most populous nation on earth. He personally solved a thousand problems a day, having to substitute in practically every matter for a timorous bureaucracy that was forever reluctant to make any decision or bear any responsibility. He dispatched the affairs of the state with the supreme efficiency of an old Taoist ruler who knows that one should govern a large empire the way one cooks a little fish. He seemingly never slept and still looked always relaxed. He could simultaneously display an exacting attention for minute details that was worthy of a fussy housewife, and a breadth of vision that awed the greatest statesmen of our time. Although he permanently occupied the center of the stage, his public activity was still a mere sinecure compared with the other show—far more intense, absorbing, and momentous—that was running nonstop offstage in the dark recesses of inner-Party politics. There he had to perform incredible acrobatics in order to remain on top of the greased pole—eliminating rivals in a relentless power struggle, dodging ambushes, surviving murderous plots hatched by old comrades, and so on. His task became more and more superhuman as he had to lend singlehandedly, for the benefit of a bemused international audience, an impressive façade of humanity, intelligence, and sanity to a regime whose increasing cruelty, ineptitude, and madness were finally to come out in the open during the last ten years of the Maoist era.

Zhou's reputation may eventually suffer from the posthumous debunking of Mao (which is a paradox, as, in the end, Mao ruthlessly attempted to get rid of him). Still, some Chinese intellectuals are now probably being unfair when they describe him as having merely played Albert Speer to Mao's Hitler. Zhou's relation to his master did not reflect a straightforward subordination; the actual situation was far more complex. For many years before Mao reached supreme power, Zhou had actually been running the Chinese Communist Party behind the screen of a series of ineffectual or unlucky nominal leaders who were purged one after another. Zhou weathered these successive crises practically unscathed; from these early days onward, he displayed an uncanny ability for political survival that was to become the hallmark of his long career. He developed methods that made him unsinkable: always exert power by proxy; never occupy the front seat; whenever the opposition is stronger, immediately yield.

His unique skills made him forever indispensable, while simultaneously he cultivated a quality of utter elusiveness; no one could pin him down to a specific political line, nor could one associate him with any particular faction. He never expressed personal ideas or indulged in penning his own theoretical views. Where did he really stand? What did he actually believe? Apparently he had no other policies but those of the leader of the moment, and nourished no other ambitions but to serve him with total dedication. Yet the brilliance of his mind, the sharpness of his intelligence, the electrifying quality of his personal magnetism, eloquence, and authority constantly belied the kind of bland selflessness that he so studiously displayed in the performance of his public duties. Zhou's engima lay in the paradox that, with all his exceptional talents, he should also present a sort of disconcerting and essential *hollowness*.

Twenty-three hundred years ago, Zhuang Zi, in giving advice to a king, made him observe that when a small boat drifts in the way of a huge barge, the crew of the barge will immediately shout abuse at the stray craft; however, coming closer, if they discover that the little boat is empty, they will simply shut up and quietly steer clear of it. He concluded that a ruler who has to sail the turbulent waters of politics should first and foremost learn how to become *an empty boat*.

History provides few examples of statesmen who were as successful as Zhou Enlai in mastering this subtle discipline. It enabled him to become the ultimate survivor. There was no limit to his willingness to compromise. Once, when the Communists had to cooperate again with the Nationalists, a local Party cadre rebelled against this shameless fraternization with fascist butchers, and indignantly asked Zhou, "Should we become mere concubines?" Zhou replied coolly, "If necessary, we should become prostitutes." Yet he was not seeking survival for survival's sake; he survived in order to win. He combined utter fluidity with absolute resilience, like water, which takes instantaneously the shape of whatever container it happens to fill, and simultaneously never surrenders one single atom of its own nature—in the end it always prevails. The contrast between the posthumous fates of Mao and Zhou is quite illuminating in this respect. Mao's mummy was left to rot in a huge and grotesque mausoleum in the heart of Peking, as if better to witness from this vantage point the dismantling of all his policies. As for Zhou, once more, he vanished into thin air—quite literally this time, since he wisely requested that his ashes be scattered over the country—and beyond his death it is still he who is ruling today over China, through his own handpicked successors.

Zhou made history for half a century and wielded enormous power over one-quarter of mankind; yet he apparently never succumbed to the temptation of self-aggrandizement and the lust for supremacy to which none of the other Chinese leaders remained immune. He withstood countless trials, crises, humiliations, and dangers; he repeatedly served, with stoic loyalty, leaders who did not have his ability or his experience; and yet he never wavered in his commitment to Chinese Communism. From where did he derive his spiritual strength? What motivated him? Like many bourgeois intellectuals of his generation, in his youth he was fired by intense patriotism. In his early twenties, while in Europe, he seems to have identified once and for all the salvation of China with the victory of Communism. We know nothing more of his spiritual evolution. Zhou's conundrum was thus compounded with a tragic irony: this man who generously dedicated himself, soul and body, to the service of China, ended up as the staunchest pillar of a regime that managed to kill more innocent Chinese citizens in twenty-five years of peace than had the combined forces of all foreign imperialists in one hundred years of endemic aggression.

■

There are three basic books on Zhou Enlai—two in English, one in Chinese. Kai-yu Hsu's is the earliest and most readable;* although the book is marred in the end by a certain maudlinism, Hsu performed remarkable detective work in tracking down and interviewing Zhou's surviving relatives, old schoolmates, and acquaintances. This enabled him to write the most detailed account

* Kai-yu Hsu, *Chou En-lai: China's Gray Eminence* (New York: Doubleday, 1968).

of Zhou's youth and early activities. Li Tien-min's work* is dry and terse, concerned less with the man than with his political activity, about which it provides clear and sound information. Yan Jingwen† combines Hsu's human and psychological approach with Li's political acumen; his book is at times too fragmented, chatty, and anecdotal, but it also offers illuminating insights. It is perhaps the most stimulating of the three.

A common shortcoming of these three works was that they were quite sketchy on the post-1949 period and could not touch at all on Zhou's dramatic final years. There is room, if not necessarily for a new biography, at least for a monograph that could update these earlier studies. I am not sure that Mr. Wilson's book‡ can fill the gap; the author probably did not even nurture such ambition. This biography is concerned merely with storytelling, not with history-writing. The first half of the book is sound enough, as it essentially duplicates its excellent predecessors, but it is not very useful. What is the point of rewriting Kai-yu Hsu's work? The reader might as well refer directly to the original.§ Yet, in all fairness, it must be said that Mr. Wilson also makes some pertinent and useful references to sources that had not been available to the earlier biographers.‖

---

* Li Tien-min, *Chou En-lai* (Taipei: Institute of International Relations, 1970).

† Yan Jingwen, *Zhou Enlai Pingzhuan* (Hongkong: Bo Wen, 1974).

‡ Dick Wilson, *Zhou Enlai: A Biography* (New York: Viking, 1984).

§ In at least one place, Mr. Wilson errs when paraphrasing an anecdote taken from Hsu's book. He unaccountably attributes to Zhou Enlai words actually pronounced by Shao Lizi (p. 81). Hsu's anecdote (also found in Yan) becomes nonsensical when retold by Wilson, who misunderstood its actual import.

‖ Whenever he leaves his three guides, however, he is treading on dangerous ground: at one point, for instance, producing a double anecdote that seems rather fanciful, he refers to a Japanese source, itself quoting a Chinese source (Nishikawa citing He Changgong—twice). Had he bothered to check directly with the Chinese source, he would have found that the two Japanese quotes were bogus.

The second half of the book (covering the post-1949 period) is disappointing; it amounts to little more than an enumeration of Zhou's public appearances. There is no real understanding of the complex dynamics of the various political struggles that took place during this eventful and dramatic era. One single example should suffice to illustrate how, as a result of Mr. Wilson's confused perception, history is being stood on its head: "Liu [Shaoqi's] pragmatism seemed now to Zhou far more dangerous because Liu appeared to be ready, under the twin pressures of economic hardship and bureaucratic conservatism, to let socialism go altogether."*

Many years ago, some twelve-year-old Red Guards earnestly believed, for one long, hot summer, that Liu Shaoqi and Deng Xiaoping were actually bent on liquidating socialism and on restoring capitalism. That in 1984 (Deng Xiaoping *regnante*!) there still can be respectable contemporary China specialists who entertain such notions should be a cause for endless wonderment.

* Wilson, *Zhou Enlai*, 237.

IS THERE LIFE
AFTER MAO?

■   ■   ■   ■   ■

I am afraid I cannot do justice to Mr. Garside's excellent
book;* my difficulty has nothing to do with the book itself, it
is simply that I find myself practically unable to write one
more line on the subject of Chinese contemporary politics. Com-
menting on the issue of Algeria in a letter to Jean Grenier, Albert
Camus wrote in 1958: "One does not write in order to say that
everything is screwed up. In such a situation one keeps silent."
To write is to hope, and what hope is there left?

When Mao was riding high on the Chinese stage—and even

* Roger Garside, *Coming Alive: China after Mao* (New York: McGraw-Hill, 1981).

higher in the minds of some Western "China experts"—for a foreign critic, debunking the Great Helmsman was an activity that could still afford some kind of grim fun. This horrible era, in its very excesses, had reached a point of absurdity that spelled its own doom. Even though outside observers could do nothing to hasten its passing, at least one could collect and record the grotesque portents of its impending collapse.

Writing became even easier for us after the fall of the Maoist Gang: the Chinese people's rejoicing was infectious and inspiring. There was a stupendous and sweeping wave of new reforms. There was a stunning outspokenness in the press, frank exposure of the crimes and disasters of the Maoist period. The new leaders—or more accurately, the old guard, which had returned to power—seemed to be sincerely committed to a bold and drastic overhaul of the regime. They daringly opened the country to the outside world. After nearly thirty years of rule by arbitrary violence and despotic whims, they promised to establish at last "socialist legality." In the wake of these new initiatives, the brief and unforgettable "Peking Spring" blossomed: the people were silent no more; young activists stepped forward, and with admirable courage, lucidity, and eloquence, they demanded human rights and democracy. However, their movement was soon suppressed; the new "socialist laws" were used to throw the democrats and the patriots in jail on trumped-up charges, after parodies of trials in front of kangaroo courts.

Yet even this dismal ending of the democratic movement could not completely quash the immense hopes that had risen from the post-Mao reforms. The explosion of truth in the officially controlled media, however brief, left indelible marks. A small number of courageous elderly and middle-aged writers who now command a large audience still seem unwilling to relinquish their newly recovered integrity, even though they are increasingly subjected to pressures and threats. Exchanges with the outside world continue to develop, at least in the educational and cultural areas (areas that, in the long run, may prove to be of decisive influence for the future of China). Because of all these factors, and even though ominous signs were already multiplying, it was still possible, one or two years ago, to share Mr. Garside's opinion that the People's Republic was engaged in a "movement from totalitarian tyranny to a system more humane, [in a] struggle to free itself from a straitjacket woven of feudalism and Marxism-Leninism." I am ill-placed to criticize Mr. Garside's conclusions; at that time, I myself said the same things.

How naïve we were!

We should have known from the beginning where post-Mao China was heading, under the leadership of these old ghosts revived from an evil past. The new "legality" was sponsored by Peng Zhen, the notorious butcher who had presided over the bloody and savage purges of the early fifties. And the entire show is run by Deng Xiaoping, who has been known for more than fifty years as an orthodox and narrow Stalinist bureaucrat. We deluded ourselves into believing that these leaders had acquired some kind of new wisdom during the period of persecution and disgrace they suffered at the time of the "Cultural Revolution." (On this subject we should have read Milan Kundera: "When I was a boy, I used to idealize the people who returned from political imprisonment. Then I discovered that most of the oppressors were former victims. The dialectics of the executioner and his victim are very complicated. To be a victim is often the best training for an executioner. The desire to punish injustice is not only a desire for justice, pure and simple, but also a subconscious desire for new evil.") When they spoke of "democracy" and "legality," they never meant to extend these guarantees and rights to the ordinary people; they merely wanted to restore *within the ruling elite* a set of rules that would enable them to play their usual games in less murderous conditions.

The only excuse for our naïveté is that, for a while, even the Chinese themselves seem to have been deluded. One should remember that there was a time, not so long ago, when Deng Xiaoping truly became the most popular personality in the entire country; the rhetoric of his Maoist enemies had nearly succeeded in persuading the people that he indeed intended "to restore capitalism." Mr. Garside's book is perhaps not fully free from some lingering influence of this early euphoria—witness, for instance, the passages dealing with Zhou Enlai, where we see this otherwise cool and competent analyst becoming uncharacteristically sentimental, as if carried away by the mythology of the time. Actually, it is not only Deng who is now seen and judged by the Chinese for what he always was—not a champion of the people, but a ruthless apparatchik for whom the unchallenged power of the ruling elite remains the first priority and the ultimate imperative. The posthumous prestige of Zhou himself is also beginning to suffer from a severe revision. In private conversations, Chinese intellectuals are quick to point out now that, for all his genuinely attractive and even fascinating talents, Zhou eventually betrayed them all, and in his relations with Mao he adopted too often the attitude of a coward and a sycophant.

Mr. Garside is most interesting in his account of events around the Democracy Wall in Peking, events that he personally witnessed. Still, on this subject, I feel that the last word should belong to Wei Jingsheng, the heroic young activist who was eventually arrested for his outspokenness and sentenced to fifteen years in prison.* Mr. Garside reports:

In speaking, Wei displayed the same boldness and clarity that marked his writing qualities. My interpretation of the way China's politics were developing differed from his in some important

* See Appendix: Wei Jingsheng, *The Fifth Modernization: Democracy.*

respects, but that was irrelevant to my purpose in meeting him—
which was to gain a better understanding of such activists. I
asked him whether he expected the Democracy movement to col-
lide with the Party leadership at some stage. "Certainly," he replied, "because we want to go further than those Party leaders
who have called for democracy and liberation of thinking."

"But those leaders have done much to show that they want
more freedom in China. Why don't you accept that they want genuine democracy?"

"Because they have been Communists all their lives."

During Mao's last years, China was sinking. Yet, for him who
drowns, to hit the bottom still yields a chance to rise again to the
surface, whereas Deng Xiaoping's rule is more akin to the aim-
less drift of a dead dog; only its belly, swollen with the windy
promises of the "Four Modernizations," still keeps it vaguely
afloat. At the end of Mao's reign there was a widespread realization that nothing could be worse, and in this feeling an odd
comfort could be found—such demented policies simply could
not last much longer, things *had* to change. Despair and hope
are fierce and closely related passions that both pertain to the
living; there seems to be little room for either in China today.
The regime is dead.*

Usually, in any field of expertise, the layman sees only uni-
formity where the informed person perceives differences. For instance, the untrained eye might confuse a Ming landscape for a
Song painting; for the connoisseur, they are worlds apart. In
Chinese contemporary politics, the reverse is true. Some time

---

* I mean it literally, but I wouldn't venture to forecast the time of its fall. As has
already been pointed out (in the third essay of this volume), Huc, traveling through
China in the 1840s, observed quite accurately that the Manchu dynasty had run
its course and was finished. Yet it took another seventy years for the old empire
actually to collapse. When operating on the scale of China, history adopts another
rhythm.

ago I witnessed this scene at a university seminar in Europe: a number of political scientists were discussing the various political shifts in the history of the People's Republic and were trying to assess the implications of the latest changes brought about by Deng Xiaoping. After they had analyzed at great length and with subtle nuances all the possible and future implications of Deng's innovations, they finally asked the opinion of a distinguished scholar who had said nothing so far, but who happened to be the only person there with genuine insight on the subject, since he himself was a Chinese and had just arrived from the People's Republic. With a smile of infinite weariness, he said simply: "Political changes? I haven't noticed any during the last thirty years. Why should we expect any in the future?"

And this is indeed the heartbreaking lesson to be drawn from the Deng Xiaoping experiment. We begin to see precisely how much and how far the system can reform itself. We have taken the exact measure of the beast's ability to change its stripes and its spots. What else is still to be expected and hoped for? The leaders have merely succeeded in ridding the regime of its Maoist faith—the dream to transform man, a vision that alone could somehow compensate for the fundamental irrationality of the system and justify to some extent all the exorbitant sacrifices it exacted from the populace. Now they begin to realize that, for better or for worse, this very dream had been providing the driving energy that could mobilize the nation and propel the country forward. They are merely left with a huge, amorphous, and inert machine—a colossal and timorous bureaucracy that becomes more and more useless and corrupt, paralyzes all initiatives, bars all the avenues of life, and cannot be budged by one inch in any direction. The Party, now cynical and completely discredited, is simply turning into a mafia of opportunists who are incompetent in all matters not directly related to their personal advancement. Lenin said that "Party members should not be measured by nar-

row standards of petit-bourgeois snobbery. Sometimes a scoundrel is useful to our Party, precisely because he is a scoundrel."
What he did not foresee was that, by the seemingly ineluctable
evolutionary law of all victorious revolutions, the courageous,
idealistic, and generous majority would progressively disappear;
since they were ready to sacrifice themselves, they were soon
sacrificed, making room for the scoundrels to take over. "One
cannot be a Communist," concluded Milovan Djilas, "and preserve one iota of one's personal integrity." Scoundrels co-opt
themselves into power; the system itself operates a selection in
reverse. It penalizes and eliminates decency, intelligence, and
sincerity while rewarding and promoting all the basest inclina-
tions: sycophancy, deviousness, lazy parroting, envy, hatred,
moral cowardice, opportunism, ability to lie, willingness to inform on others, to denounce and to betray even one's closest
friends, one's own blood. On top of this, add the fact that the
Party cadres of today suffered tremendously during the "Cultural
Revolution." They returned to power with one single driving obsession: to get even, to make up for all their losses, to enjoy their
luck to the full while it lasts. (They have little faith in the future.
If the rats are not yet abandoning ship, at least they are busy
securing the escape of their progeny. A great number of high-
ranking officials are now taking advantage of their positions to
send their children abroad, often without intending them to return.) They cling desperately to their privileges, unwilling to take
the slightest initiative, since any initiative entails risks. The
problem is not simply that they do nothing, but that they efficiently prevent any useful activity that more talented subordinates might be tempted to launch. Personal integrity, intellectual
creativity, imagination, competence, and expertise appear to
them as so many challenges and potential threats to their authority. The tabula rasa that the "Cultural Revolution" established in all areas of culture, intelligence, and learning was

meant as a radical measure to protect the power of an incompetent and half-literate ruling class; what happened later in the
Cambodia of Pol Pot was basically a cruder and simpler application of the same principles.

What place do ordinary people occupy in this picture? A skill
that the Chinese developed to the utmost also proved to be their
curse—the art of survival. A proverbial saying tragically summarized centuries of political wisdom: "Rather be a dog in a time
of peace than a man in a time of disorder." This traditional attitude may partly explain how such a talented nation could repeatedly accommodate itself to various forms of autocracy and
despotism; still, it cannot fully account for the much more complex relationship that exists now between the Chinese and their
Communist rulers.

Custine's famous observation on Tsarist Russia ("*Un peuple
opprimé a toujours mérité sa peine; la tyrannie est l'oeuvre des
nations, pas le chef-d'oeuvre d'un homme*"*) was perhaps too
extreme. Yet, today Alexander Zinoviev has given a new development to this notion in his brilliant and disquieting para-
doxes on Stalinism: his contention that Stalin's power was the
ultimate expression of *the people's power* could be applied even
more convincingly to Mao. These views have disturbing implications; for instance, they directly challenge Solzhenitsyn's simplistic and reassuring dichotomy of evil *Soviet* leaders oppressing
saintly and innocent Russians.

In China the current situation is even more intricate. The
"Cultural Revolution" was a civil war that was prevented from
running its full course. It is currently estimated by the Chinese
themselves that nearly *a hundred million* people were to some
extent directly involved in the violence of the "Cultural Revo-

* "Oppressed people always deserve their fate; tyranny is achieved by a whole nation, it is not the accomplishment of a single individual."

lution"—either as active participants or as victims. More than ninety percent of the people who committed crimes during that period—murder, torture, looting—remain unpunished. The problem is not that they were not identified; on the contrary, it is simply that there are too many of them. In most cases, they were quietly reinstalled in their former positions. Since the bitterest fighting and the worst atrocities generally took place between rival factions within the walls of particular "units" (administrations, factories, schools, etc.), now it is not rare to see murderers sharing the same office or the same cramped living quarters with the close relatives, associates, and friends of their victims. People who have been beaten up, denounced, betrayed, and sent to jail by their own colleagues or subordinates have to work again with them, side by side, day after day, as if nothing had ever happened between them.

If totalitarianism were merely the persecution of an innocent nation by a small group of tyrants, overthrowing it would still be a relatively easy matter. Actually, the extraordinary resilience of the system resides precisely in its ability to associate the victims themselves with the all-pervasive organization and management of terror, to make them participate in the crimes of their executioners, to turn them into active collaborators and accomplices. In this way the victims acquire a personal stake in the defense and preservation of the very regime that is torturing and crushing them. To the survivors of the "Cultural Revolution"—and, in a sense, today every adult Chinese is such a survivor—one could apply what Leszek Kolakowski said of the survivors of the Soviet camps: "Even those who somehow survived the camps nevertheless acquired a subconscious interest in supporting the Communist lie because *they had themselves assisted in creating it.*"

The festering abscess of the "Cultural Revolution" is now merely hidden from sight rather than being effectively treated. This results in an explosive situation, made all the more dangerous by the failure of the regime to carry out any fundamental reform. Immobility is not stability; by becoming petrified, a structure is not made strong but brittle. To understand Communist China, the insights offered by Eastern European and Russian dissenters on the subject of the USSR are often more enlightening than the specialized analysis of many Pekinologists. Talking of the Soviet Union, Kolakowski pointed out: "If the Soviet leaders suspected for one moment that the Western world knew what *they* know about their system, their worries about the staying power of the Soviet empire would increase immeasurably." How much more accurately the same could be said of the People's Republic! Recently in Hong Kong I had the chance to share lodgings with a remarkable visiting scholar from Peking. Every morning he used to rush to the newspapers—"to check" he said sardonically, "if the People's Republic has not collapsed during the night!"

China under Communism appears more and more like a dead planet; it is on a steady orbit, but the very nature of its political atmosphere prevents any kind of growth, and even seems to preclude the emergence of life; yet it will pursue its sterile and immutable course—till a random collision makes it explode.

POSTSCRIPT

Since the writing of this article in 1981, there has been a fairly spectacular relaxation of the death grip that socialism exerts over the Chinese economy, especially in the countryside. However, these economic policies will appear new only to those who ignore the historical mirror of the Soviet experience: the Russians already tried these various recipes many years ago, and thus, if we

wish to forecast the future of the Chinese reforms, we ought perhaps first to read again Jean-François Revel's summing-up of the
Khrushchevite experiment:

The bureaucracy pushed Khrushchev aside, because in order
to revive the economy, he attacked the Party monopoly by setting
up regional committees for agriculture and industry. In doing
this, he deprived regional secretaries and other Party apparat-
chiks of their local omnipotence, and thus of their main source
of profits. The Establishment might not tolerate it. Every attempt
to liberate a Communist economy could be compared to a potato-
sack race. Once the participants reach a certain speed, they cannot accelerate further, unless they drop their sacks, i.e., get rid
of the Party and its monopoly on decision-making, which is the
very essence of the regime. This would amount to a revolution!
When things reach such a point, the Party applies the brakes and
there is a return to central planning, which means stagnation and
regression.*

* Jean-François Revel, *Le Rejet de l'Etat* (Paris: Grasset, 1984), 108.

PEKING AUTUMN

■   ■   ■   ■   ■

I n Chekhov's letters, there is one passage where the writer gives some advice to an actor who is taking, in one of his plays, the part of a desperate man. As this actor had a tendency to overplay the character—screaming, wringing his hands, rolling tragic eyes—Chekhov made him observe that a man who is truly experiencing despair keeps very quiet and merely stands by the window, whistling softly.

The Chinese have known for ages this esthetic principle of "less is more"; actually, they brought it to an extreme degree of refinement. The expressive understatement has become one of their main literary and pictorial devices. In Chinese poetry, for

instance, one can find a good example of this in a famous short
poem by Xin Qiji (twelfth century); the piece is sublime, take my
word for it, but it would need a poet to translate it, and I can
merely offer a prose paraphrase. The poet first explains how, in
his youth, when he had not yet tasted sorrow, he loved to strike
romantic postures, climbing on high balconies from whence he
would sing imaginary sorrows that he invented for himself in order to compose new poems. But now, as life has eventually made
him empty the bitter cup of sorrow to its last dregs, he refrains
from talking   or, if he has to speak, he merely says (and this is
the last verse of the poem): "The weather is cool, what a beautiful
autumn!"

   If you wish to hear the latest news of the beautiful Peking autumn, read Yang Jiang's *A Cadre School Life: Six Chapters.**
Yang Jiang is a very distinguished old lady, a playwright who
translated Cervantes into Chinese. She is the wife of Qian Zhongshu, a famous scholar and writer, arguably one of the greatest
minds of our age. At the end of the "Cultural Revolution," like
all their academic colleagues whose crime was to be intelligent
and educated, Yang and Qian were forcibly separated and sent
to the countryside. In the political context of the time, and considering their age and frail health, it was reasonable to expect
that they would die while breaking stones and carting manure.
But another whim of the authorities brought both of them back
to Peking two years later; furthermore, the unpredictable course
of Chinese politics was eventually to allow Yang Jiang to write

* Excellently translated by Geremie Barmé with the assistance of Bennett Lee (Hong
Kong: Joint Publishing Co., 1982), it was published in the United States, Canada,
and the United Kingdom in 1984 by Joint Publishing Co. in association with Readers International of New York and London. Another translation made by Howard
Goldblatt is quite good too, but it was published under the rather unfortunate title
Six Chapters of My Life Downunder (Seattle: University of Washington Press,
1984), thus seemingly implying that Yang was transported to Australia—which
would not have been such a bad fate after all!

and to publish an account of her deportation, eight years after these events.

These *Six Chapters* are written with elegant simplicity. The author talks softly, with a touch of humor, without ever raising her voice. She tells of the modest misfortunes and humble happinesses that formed, against a background of mud and misery, the everyday fabric of her exile. In a jail, the minutest accidents of life acquire a flavor and a significance that, in our careless freedom, we hardly perceive anymore. Philip Roth, talking about Eastern Europe, accurately described this situation: "In the West everything goes and nothing matters; there, nothing goes and everything matters."

This slim little booklet is easily read in one sitting. Paradoxically, it is also heavy with all that it does *not* say. Its weight cannot be solely explained by the peculiar density that every object, each incident acquires in the emptiness of captivity; it is also the product of a massive understatement. Yang Jiang, of course, is one of those subtle artists who know how to say less in order to express more, but in her case, this esthetic reserve is further reinforced by a political taboo. We should remember that the People's Republic of China has invented the ultimate form of censorship—a censorship that is not enforced by any specialized agencies (which do not even exist in China), but, in a way that is far more economical and efficient, its responsibility is directly entrusted to every writer individually.

Yang Jiang lived through a disaster whose magnitude paralyzes the imagination. Yet, today in China, it would be dangerous for anyone to attempt to explore the origins and the implications of this catastrophe. The lunatic decision taken by Mao to carry out a mass deportation of all intellectuals on the sole ground that they were intellectuals (more than 20 million people were affected by this order) has probably no equivalent in all history, if we except of course the deportation of the Jews by the

Nazis, and the deportation of the educated population of the Cambodian cities by the Khmer Rouge (the latter, by the way, were consciously trying to emulate the Maoist model).

Yang Jiang deliberately limits her narrative to her own narrow, individual experience, and this experience itself is never described in full, but merely suggested through a series of fragmentary, disconnected notations, sketched with sparse brushstrokes. The broader context of collective madness in which her ordeal took place is only hinted at; we accidentally glimpse its oblique refraction here and there, but never confront it face to face. To put it in theatrical terms, the only backdrop of the *Six Chapters* consists of the tiny setting in which the author believed for a while that she would have to spend the rest of her life; all that we see onstage is a lame wooden bed in a crowded hut, loaded with all her wretched belongings, like the raft of a shipwreck; or again, a muddy corner of the vegetable garden where she tried so hard to grow a few turnips—which the starving peasants of the neighborhood would steal even before they had the time to mature.

Only a few characters cross this familiar little world. Luckily, her husband is living in a neighboring camp. Sometimes the old lovers can take advantage of their everyday drudgery to meet clandestinely and chat for a few minutes behind a hedge. The real action unfolds entirely outside the book. From time to time, indirectly, we hear remote rumbles and muffled shouts that rise from backstage. The news that a beloved relative or a close colleague has just committed suicide is disclosed as if by accident—it is put apologetically between parentheses, and yet these ominous echoes are enough to remind us of the existence of this invisible outside world that is sinking into terror and lunacy. However, the author always cuts short these allusions and returns at once to the touching and ridiculous little happenings of everyday camp life: the misadventure of the old poet who dropped a bar of soap in the soup; how the inmates built their latrines only to see them immediately looted by the local peasants; how the author adopted a puppy and was then forced to abandon it.

Yang Jiang's exquisite art certainly had no need for official recognition. Yet the Communist authorities saw fit to commend her achievement solemnly; they extolled it as an example to follow, as (in their own words) her book "shows a wound, yet utters no complaint." Indeed. This last stroke brings irresistibly to mind one of the most bitterly Chinese of all political anecdotes:

In the Tang dynasty, the younger brother of an official prepares to leave for his first posting. He promises his elder brother that he will be utterly circumspect and patiently obedient in all his dealings with his superiors: "If they spit on me, I shall simply wipe my face without a word." "Oh, no!" replies the elder brother, terrified. "They might take your gesture for an impudence. Let the spittle dry by itself." This utterance has entered the common language as a proverb (*tuo mian zi gan*); it describes a reality that remains very much alive today, and Yang Jiang's quiet smile can provide one of its latest and most heartbreaking illustrations.

· Hygiene

THE DOUBLE
VISION OF
HAN SUYIN

On the Character of a Trimmer

■ "After all, people can change, can't they?"
—MAO ZEDONG*

■   ■   ■   ■   ■

Madame Han Suyin is very popular in the West. In China (except among some bureaucrats of the Propaganda Department) she is unloved, and nowadays most Chinese intellectuals, artists, and writers will frown if you so much as mention her name. Is this an excessively harsh response on the part of the survivors of the "Cultural Revolution"? The publi-

---

* I found this quotation from Mao *not* in the selected works of the Great Teacher, but in a book by Madame Han Suyin. Since Madame Han Suyin is more than casual toward facts (as some of her hapless acquaintances discovered when finding themselves described in her memoirs), I suggest that this particular Thought of Mao be taken with a good pinch of salt.

177

cation of her latest book, *My House Has Two Doors* (New York: G. P. Putnam's Sons, 1980), provides the opportunity to answer this question through a retrospective examination of her work.

Madame Han Suyin likes to take her imagery from the natural world, and many of her books have fine titles: *And the Rain My Drink* (1956), *The Mountain Is Young* (1958), *The Morning Deluge* (1972), and so on. In attempting to put her latest book into perspective, I was inquisitive enough to leaf through a few of her other recent publications: *China in the Year 2001* (New York: Basic Books, 1967), *Asia Today* (Montreal–London, 1969), and *Wind in the Tower* (Boston: Little, Brown, 1976). (In the passages quoted below I have retranscribed the Chinese names into *pinyin*, and abbreviated the references to *Doors*, *2001*, *Asia*, and *Wind*, respectively.) During those hours of reading I often found myself floundering, almost drowning in the roaring tide of the author's powerful imagination, but at the same time I acquired a firmer grasp of the positively *cosmic* quality of her overall vision. It is a fertile chaos, a polyphonic coexistence of opposites, a lyrical alternance, a grand dialogue between Yin and Yang. After all, Madame Han Suyin has readily informed us that her house has two doors, and her work resembles those clothes you can buy with two different patterns and colors, so that, depending on your mood or the weather, you can wear them with the outside in or the inside out. I believe that in the trade such clothing is called "reversible"—a useful notion, especially for people fond of turning their coats. Her work, thus, displays two different faces simultaneously, heads as well as tails; the subtle counterpoint can only be properly appreciated if one takes the trouble to put them into stereoscopic focus. A number of examples follow.

Heads

The great emphasis, in this revolution, [is] on the use of reason, criticism, debate, and not on force. (*2001*, p. 193) What is sought is not the physical punishment of the evildoers, but awareness, rallying and unity. . . . This experiment bears watching. (*2001*, p.200) Through the Great Cultural Revolution, the remaking of man is being attempted for one-quarter of the world. . . . It is Mao Zedong who has seen the problem in its universal terms, the Remaking of Man. (*2001*, p.246)

Tails

Passing through the street, I catch sight, here and there, of barbed wire atop walls. Probably temporary prisons. Each organization, factory, university has its own detention area. (*Doors*, p.513) In the ensuing "investigation sessions" [Luo Ruiqing] was pushed—so it is alleged—through a window, and his leg was broken. He received no medical care for this injury. He was carried to his public humiliation in January 1967, in a large basket, and had to crawl on the floor, dragging his broken leg behind him. . . . He Long was treated most savagely. He was diabetic and was refused medical care. He was beaten regularly being first wrapped in a blanket so that the welts would not show. (*Doors*, p.462) Xia Yan was beaten, his leg broken, and he was refused medical care. (*Doors*, p.471)

Heads

The surprise of the year 1968 was to see Chinese techniques take entirely original forms and realize, even with the Cultural Revolution and its upheavals in process, standards equivalent to, or higher than, those in international use. (*Asia*, p.102)

Tails

Phenomenal innovations are announced, all proclaimed to be the result of the Cultural Revolution. But I know that a good many were started before the Cultural Revolution . . . all of them are claimed to be due to workers' ingenuity, but I know that most of them are due to scientists. (*Doors*, p.508)

Heads

Far from being an absurdity proceeding from madness or authoritarianism, the Great Proletarian Cultural Revolution is a logical, needful, necessary event, the only way . . . to give the working class the leadership, to give the masses the largest possible democratic voice. (*Asia*, p.71)

Tails

How was it possible to remain sane with the perpetual noise, the blaring and the shouting and the screaming and the singing? (*Doors*, p.422) I was extremely nervous, and suffered from fits of depression because of the Cultural Revolution. . . . (*Doors*, p.477) In July and August 1967, everything seemed to go crazy in China. (*Doors*, p.480) The Mayor, Vice-Mayor and Party officials of Shanghai were hauled to criticism meetings, paraded through the city. . . . All over China such displays took place, designed to strike terror. . . . The writer Zhao Shuli was taken from village to village through the northwest. . . . He died of the ordeal. *And all that in the name of democracy.** (*Doors*, pp.461–62)

Heads

And for those who still think that there will be "Stalinist" purges and liquidations, I now quote from *The Red Flag:* "Even diehard

---

* Sentences in italics appear only in the French version, *La Moission du phénix*, p. 83.

capitalist-roaders should be allowed a way out. . . ." A way out, in the great tradition of Chinese humanism. No liquidations, no massive purges. . . . (*Asia*, pp. 73–74)

Tails

There were figures of 90,000 casualties in Sichuan and a good many too in Yunnan. Guangzhou was ugly with summary executions by rival factions. . . . (*Wind*, pp. 316–17) "A reign of gratuitous terror—horrifying," said others. In every city and quarter it was different: from harassment to murder, from endless interrogation to beating to death. By October, in Peking alone, 86,000 "counterrevolutionaries" had been discovered. In Shanghai 400,000 "bourgeois and capitalists" were removed from their houses. (*Doors*, p. 456)

Heads

Of course [the Cultural Revolution] was grueling . . . a number of mistakes were made . . . but taken all in all, it is certain that violence was not condoned, nor was it on the large scale which Western reports made it out to be. . . . (*Asia*, p. 72) It fell to Jiang Qing to denounce the Ultra-Left, and she was the first to do so. . . . Jiang Qing was the deputy head of the Cultural Revolution Group, in no sense responsible for their depredations, for she was the first to fight against them. . . . (*Wind*, pp. 316–17)

Tails

Jiang Qing's speech to the Red Guards in Peking on 22 June 1967 aroused unprecedented fighting . . . and provoked many deaths. (*Moisson*, p. 168)* [Jiang Qing] then used a phrase which

* This paragraph, which should appear on p. 513 of *Doors*, was deleted from the English edition and is to be found only in the French version.

. . . was the green light for continued violence, at a time when the Red Guards were attacking army garrisons and raiding arsenals. (*Doors*, p.475)

Heads

Direct collision between China and the U.S.A. is now almost inevitable; the military-industrial complex of the U.S.A. wants to attack, to drop the first bomb on China. This will be the signal for "total war which knows no boundaries." (*2001*, p.170)

Tails

There would not be a war between America and China now. Mao's faith that the two peoples, the Americans and the Chinese, would inevitably become friends again one day, expressed so often through the years, had now seen fruition. (*Wind*, pp.366–67)

Heads

The Great Proletarian Cultural Revolution tries to abolish servility and unthinking obedience, docile tools and slavishness. "Dare to think, to act and criticize." Not 700 million docile tools, but 700 million original thinkers, "700 Million Mao Zedongs" is the aim. (*Asia*, p.71) The core of the problem of building a socialist economy *without exploitation* . . . is to change the content of motivation, to provide, through continuous and painstaking socialist education, through rectification campaigns and movements, a change in behavior "within the soul of man." This conversion has been attempted before, in religious systems, but not with the thoroughness of a science, which is Mao Zedong's treatment of this psychological remaking. (*2001*, pp.185–186)

Tails

"I'll go crazy if I see one more Mao religious service," said Richard Hung to me. . . . [He] had come upon a dawn ceremony—a courtyard full of people swinging their bodies in ecstasy in front of a large portrait of Mao Zedong. This was the morning invocation, asking Chairman Mao for directives: rocking of the body, chanting, dancing with "offer hearts," gestures, calling upon Mao in a litany of praise ("great, great, great") for his orders for the day. Then there was the opening of the little red book, and the quotation on the page fallen upon was the answer. . . . "It's like the Holy Rollers and consulting the Bible for answers and the Moral Rearmament People who speak to God," said Richard. He did not think he could put up with it any longer. (*Doors*, p. 497)

Heads

Lin Biao's appearance does not indicate a military takeover but the continuation of the revolutionary tradition, in which it is the function of the People's Liberation Army to "train cadres and successors of the Revolution." . . . The possibility of a revisionist coup against Mao's leadership was removed by Lin Biao reasserting the political and ideological primacy of Mao Zedong Thought in the army. The Chinese, therefore, do not regard the ascension of Lin Biao as a takeover but as the reassertion of ideological primacy over purely military ambitions. (*2001*, pp. 191–92)

Tails

Five out of the thirteen military regions were under Lin Biao's appointees. . . . Six of his followers and his wife, Ye Qun, were

ensconced in the Military Affairs Committee. He had a web of
his own appointees in some important revolutionary committees.
There was a dominance of military personnel in the Central Committee. . . . (*Wind*, p.341) Lin Biao's short dominance represented a tendency ingrained in the minds of the Chinese people:
the acceptance of authoritarianism (*Wind*, p.376) The Lin Biao
affair pinpointed the danger of recrudescent warlordism. (*Wind*,
p.377) Lin Biao, his wife, Ye Qun, and son . . . [began] the plot
to launch a military coup d'état, and perhaps to assassinate
Mao. . . . (*Wind*, p.346)

Heads

The role of the People's Liberation Army during the Cultural
Revolution has been very important. The army was given the following orders: If hit, do not retaliate; if shot at, do not fire back;
and do not lose your temper under any circumstances. . . . Because the soldiers never fired at any group (though at times shot
at by saboteurs . . .) the Liberation Army earned for itself an
extremely high level of awareness and performance. (*Asia*,
pp.68–69)

Tails

But in May 1968 in China the People's Liberation Army had been
empowered to shoot down those who refused to relinquish their
weapons . . . From May to July, grim and bloody battles were
fought. . . . Some commanders, however, did not exhibit much
tender care for the young. The mopping-up operations they undertook, while they heartened the population, were certainly
tough upon errant Red Guards. (*Doors*, pp.481–82) Huang
Yongsheng, the military commander [of Guangzhou], harshly
suppressed Red Guards who called him "the butcher of Guangzhou." (*Wind*, pp.316–17)

Heads

The Red Guards at one time so luridly described in the West were . . . to educate themselves, to reason, to debate. . . . Their contribution was great and significant; they unearthed many agents of the Kuomintang and some spies, caches of bullion and weapons. (*Asia*, pp.64–65)

Tails

A team of Red Guards came to investigate [my friends, the Peis]. . . . "I nearly went through the window," said Mrs. Pei when at last she talked to me, in 1975. "I begged them to let me die. What did they want, what did they want? Why were we treated in this way . . .? They said we had returned [to China] to spy." (*Doors*, pp.457–58) Other relatives of Hualan have died; two of them, husband and wife, committing suicide. They were called traitors; accused of "collusion with the outside," beaten. . . . It is quite a miracle that Hualan was not ill-treated because of me. . . . I walked the small lanes of Peking . . . immediately, children ran to announce my coming to the street committee, and people came to stare at me. Spy mania. (*Doors*, p.493) Band after band of Red Guards came down our street. . . . [A neighbor] "told the Red Guards that we had foreign goods, and they turned up everything in our house, dug up the floors and the garden, chipped the plaster off the walls to uncover gold pieces or documents. They took away books, pictures, vases, anything 'old' or 'foreign,' and also a table and a cupboard." (*Doors*, p.457)

Heads

Everyone praised the [Red Guards] whose conduct was excellent . . . and who were very clean, well-behaved and polite. . . . To pinpoint a few cases of bad conduct is to ignore the discipline and good example of the great majority of these youngsters. . . . Never had China been so exuberant, so alive, so full of the sound of drums and cymbals and so colorful . . . The Red Guards were not allowed to carry weapons nor to arrest or try anyone. . . . The Red Guards performed a task no one else could have; they literally spring-cleaned the cities. . . . (*Wind*, p.292)

Tails

There were so many absurd and ugly things being done, like the trials in Shanghai of cadres supposed to have committed adultery, who were beaten on the buttocks by self-appointed youthful judges. (*Doors*, p.458) The brutalities inflicted upon hapless individuals during June and the first part of July [1966] were nothing compared to what happened when the Lin Biao–Jiang Qing alliance won the struggle in August . . . [in the universities] we saw the teachers sweeping the grounds, cleaning the water closets and the kitchens. Some wore dunce's caps and others were abused as freaks and monsters. (*Doors*, p.431)

Heads

The Red Guards . . . learn democracy by applying democratic methods of reason and debate. (*2001*, p.200) [The Red Guards movement], therefore, was no hasty impulsive action, opening the gates to "hooliganism," as reported so erroneously in the Western press. (*2001*, p.189)

Tails

But the worst [of the Red Guards] not only burnt books and destroyed historic monuments; they also killed and tortured. (*Doors*, p.458) "The Red Guards . . . came to get [Ho]. They took turns beating him in the courtyard. . . . Then they took him away in a truck to the Western Hills where they kept their prisoners. I never saw him again. I don't know why they singled him out. Sometimes it was all so capricious." (*Doors*, p.457) In the general disruption of order the cities' jails were opened and criminals released. . . . "They did terrible things . . . if some of us learnt to torture people and to rape, it was they who incited us to do it." (*Doors*, pp.468–69)

Heads

The situation at the close of 1966 during the full blossoming of the great Proletarian Cultural Revolution was described as follows: "A vigorous and lively political situation initiated by comrade Mao Zedong is taking shape throughout our country, in which there are both centralism and democracy, both discipline and freedom, both unity of will and *personal ease of mind*." . . . This unprecedented and massive experiment is . . . China's way of preparing herself for the future . . . to go on building, as fast as possible, a socialist system which will provide both material security for the millions, and a freedom of spirit which also has never existed in the past millennia. (*2001*, pp.203–204)

Tails

The neighborhood atmosphere had changed—it was hostile. And always in the common courtyard there would be one or other member of the street committee watching us. . . . After I had left, Third Uncle's rooms might have been searched. . . . Third Uncle sat in a frightening calm, his body all gathered together, coiled upon the fear at its core. (*Doors*, p.449) Throughout my Manchurian travels I was not left alone, except at night in my bedroom. Even if I went to the toilet, in some factories and communes, a girl worker would come along with me, and watch me.

(*Doors*, p.503) [An overseas Chinese teacher told me]: "I saw [the Red Guards] come for me. I was paralyzed . . . I could do nothing but open the door for them. For six weeks they stayed with me in relays, group after group, questioning me; night and day and day and night . . . I slept no more than two or three hours a night because they woke me up to question me . . . why had I so many Western friends?" (*Doors*, pp.456–57)

Heads

The Cultural Revolution is also an enormous spurt to production, to the development of productive forces along socialist lines, for it liberates the innovating spirit of millions, instead of holding them in uncomprehending docility. . . . A new leap forward can be expected, bringing greater acceleration to the development of the economic base. (*Asia*, p.70) In terms of practical economics the Cultural Revolution produces and provides the revolutionary impetus necessary for the accomplishment of the economic breakthrough during the period of the Third Five-Year Plan (1966–70). . . . An upsurge in production has been reported in the first months of its inception. This second leap envisages . . . another speeding-up of development, to promote an even greater economic growth rate. . . . (*2001*, pp.201–02)

Tails

Throughout the months since that fateful August of 1966 Zhou [Enlai] had striven to minimize disruption. He had forbidden the interference of the Red Guards with communes and with factories . . . "revolution must stimulate production, not destroy it." But in November, he seems to have lost out on this point. . . . (*Doors*, p.464) In February [1967], at a high-level meeting presided over by Zhou Enlai, Marshal Ye Jianying and other veterans of the

Long March protested at the shambles being created. . . . By then almost all the ministers in charge of production were being denounced or hauled away to kangaroo courts held by Red Guards. The Coal Minister would die of a heart attack under the verbal abuse he endured. (*Doors*, p.466) Not all the factories were working, and in those I saw, about one-third of the machinery was idle. When I pointed to the empty benches, I was told that the workers were "resting" or that "we have fulfilled our quotas for the month," which meant that the workers had not turned up, or that raw material for processing had run out, or that the machines needed repairing. . . . I was not impressed by the young workers. They dawdled and smoked in small groups in the workshops; they played basketball in the courtyards; they loafed on the streets. (*Doors*, p.485) The young workers do not exhibit any discipline. I find dozens of them loafing about in the park with their girlfriends. (*Doors*, p.499) In Shenyang . . . the walls of factories are pockmarked with traces of bullets. Gaunt, roofless structures reach upward, as after a bombing. There is litter, and cinders; burnt down plants. (*Doors*, p.502) The steel plant of Anshan has been badly mauled. Large machinery sprawls in despair on the ground, surrounded by squatting workers trying to repair it. (*Doors*, p.504) In Lanzhou the Cultural Revolution has been grim and fearful. "The workers in the factories shot at each other," says [our official guide]. (*Doors*, p.546) In Loyang the tractor factory is a mess. Screws and bolts and spare parts of every description litter the floor in untidy heaps; the engineer who takes me around . . . says, "Our production is not too good." Of all the disciplines, only archaeology has never been obstructed during the Cultural Revolution. (*Doors*, p.611)

■

Instead of simply admiring the kaleidoscopic, shimmering texture created by these interwoven contradictions, the more petty-minded viewer may ask the reason for it. Madame Han Suyin's own answer to this question is yet again a splendidly manifold thing.

"In any circumstance, see how the wind blows, and never, never stick your neck out," she wisely recorded in her notes (*Doors*, p.495). Maoist policy is full of twists and turns, "but still, I managed. Life had never been a smooth tarred road, but a brusque and capricious river, and one learns about canoeing in wayward water" (*Doors*, p.522). Obviously, Madame Han Suyin is a seasoned mariner. Having been quick to observe that "during the last two decades China has not ceased to prove every pronouncement uttered about her false" (*2001*, p.2), she no doubt reached the sensible conclusion that if one accompanied every statement by a directly contrary statement, one was mathematically certain of being right at least half the time. And in any case, truth is a situational matter. "But I know you have not lied," she tells friends who have told her lies. "The human capacity for self-persuasion is infinite. The human soul is an assembly of contradictions. And therefore both of your versions, the one of those years, and the one you give today, are correct" (*Doors*, p.485).

We may assess the reliability of Madame Han Suyin in the same spirit as Mark Twain boasted about his own strength of character when he insisted that giving up smoking was the easiest thing in the world—he'd done it a hundred times already. Thus she is consistently loyal to everybody and anybody, providing that they are safely in power. She was loyal to Chiang Kai-shek and then to Mao Zedong, to Liu Shaoqi and then to Lin Biao, to Jiang Qing and then to Hua Guofeng—and we may be sure she is loyal before the event to whoever replaces Hua Guofeng, no matter who it is, so thoroughly has loyalty to established authority become second nature to her. If, in the thick of this absorbing exercise, she comes to the point of totally overlooking

the fate of the Chinese people, and even of actually censoring
their cries, then we must clearly excuse her, because, you see,
in Asia there is no credence to be given to the hubbub rising from
the masses: "Especially in feudal Asian countries, where the gap
between fact and fiction, truth and lies, is so very small" (*Doors*,
p. 473). So the safest approach is to stick to the official commu-
niqués provided by the currently ensconced editorial staff of the
Beijing Review.

Only political simpletons will be scandalized by her passing
on the propaganda of the "Gang of Four" in the West when the
Gang was going strong, only to switch to supporting Comrade
Deng, now that he has the wind behind him. No, the amazing
thing is their amazement. After all, it is more than two thousand
years since Sima Qian immortalized the phenomenon in a superb
passage in his *Records of the Historian*. After a period of disgrace, Lian Po, famous general of the kingdom of Zhao, was restored to the sovereign's favor. "At the moment of his disgrace
all his clients had abandoned him; once he was restored to his
command they came back to him. 'Get out,' he shouted, and one
of them replied: 'Come, sir, let us be men of our times. Surely
you must know that it is the law of the market that governs human
relations? You fall into disgrace and we leave you; you regain the
king's favor and we return to serve you. It is as simple as that—
nothing to make a fuss about.' "

Yet there are occasions when Madame Han Suyin is overcome
by a fit of unwarranted modesty, when she confesses to an ignorance we may find it difficult to credit: "But it was impossible
at the time [1969] (and would be impossible for some years, in
fact until the end of 1976) to obtain definite, hard-core information on what had happened, although I did my best" (*Doors*,
pp. 482–83).

So this particularly gifted, particularly well-informed woman,
with her privilege of unrestricted entry and direct access to the

Chinese leadership, knew less than poor drudges like L. Ladany, Simon Leys, Jacques Guillermaz, Ivan and Miriam London, and others (the names are cited in chronological order) who, on the basis of mere scrutiny of the Chinese press or interviews with refugees, managed between 1971 and 1973 to publish the gist of what she claims to have learned only this late in the day. If Madame Han Suyin had kept this up, she might almost have convinced us that we were geniuses at observation. Unfortunately, what she tells us today happens to include decisive experiences and facts that she admits having already collected in China as early as 1966 and 1969—but that did not inhibit her from writing two or three books and even more magazine articles in the same period, presenting the exact opposite of what she already knew. But in reply to this, she now alleges her worries about endangering the members of her family living in China. This is a noble concern, and one shared by thousands of Chinese living abroad—but these same Chinese have proved that there were many honorable solutions to the problem, the simplest and most usual being not to write effusive books about the "Cultural Revolution." Of course, that would raise the further problem that those profit-minded bourgeois publishers in the West are not known to pay royalties on silence.

Madame Han Suyin will undoubtedly (and rightly) complain that I have an inferior grasp of dialectics: "It is impossible to explain, or try to explain, the historical processes in China in the twentieth century, and the thought of Mao Zedong, without referring to dialectics. . . ." (Asia, p.34). Dialectics, the performing art that has given this century's intellectual circus some of its most breathtaking feats of acrobatics, must obviously be the very technique to explain the daring somersaults of the Thoughts of Madame Han Suyin. Dialectically speaking, it was she who was right to be wrong, whereas it is we who are wrong to be right.

In any case, the media-sociologists and other experts who investigate the machinery of mass communications would certainly benefit from a study of this odd phenomenon: when has such an authoritative reputation been based on such a shifting standpoint? The sole constant factor in her work is the faithfulness with which events have confuted her analyses and forecasts at every turn. This paradox—so solid a reputation built on such a slippery foundation—tends to bear out the old bewilderment once voiced by Henry de Montherlant: "In the main, people do not read; if they read, they do not understand. And those who understand forget."

THE CHINA
EXPERTS

■   ■   ■   ■   ■

P aris taxi drivers are notoriously sophisticated in their use of invective. *"Hé, va donc, structuraliste!"* is one of their recent apostrophes—which makes one wonder when they will start calling their victims "China Experts"!

Perhaps we should not be too harsh on these experts: the fraternity recently suffered a traumatic experience and is still in a state of shock. Should fish suddenly start to talk, I suppose that ichthyology would also have to undergo a dramatic revision of its basic approach. A certain type of "instant sinology" was indeed based on the assumption that the Chinese people were as different from us in their fundamental aspirations, and as unable to communicate with us, as the inhabitants of the oceanic depths; and when they eventually rose to the surface and began to cry out sufficiently loudly and clearly for their message to get through to the general public, there was much consternation among the China pundits.

Professor Edward Friedman, a teacher of Chinese Politics at an American university, recently wrote a piece in *The New York Times* that informed its readers that various atrocities had taken place in China during the Maoist era. That a professor of Chinese Politics should appear to have discovered these facts nearly ten years after even lazy undergraduates were aware of them may have made them news only for *The New York Times*; nevertheless, there was something genuinely touching in his implied confession of ignorance.

Madame Han Suyin, who knows China inside out, seldom lets her intelligence, experience, and information interfere with her writing. One rainy Sunday I amused myself by compiling a small anthology of her pronouncements on China (see the preceding essay, "The Double Vision of Han Suyin"), and learned that the "Cultural Revolution" was a "Great Leap Forward" for mankind, and that it was an abysmal disaster for the Chinese; that the Red Guards were well-behaved, helpful, and democratic-minded, and that they were savage and terrifying fascist bullies; that the "Cultural Revolution" was a tremendous spur for China's economy, and that it utterly ruined China's economy; that Lin Biao was the bulwark of the Revolution, and that Lin Biao was a murderous warlord and traitor; that Jiang Qing tried hard to prevent violence, and that Jiang Qing did her best to foster violence.

Professor Friedman and Madame Han Suyin represent the two extremes of a spectrum—the first one apparently in a state of blissful ignorance, the other knowing everything—yet the way in which both eventually stumbled suggests that, in this matter at least, the knowledge factor is, after all, quite irrelevant. What a successful China Expert needs, first and foremost, is not so much China expertise as expertise at being an Expert. Does this mean that accidental competence in Chinese affairs could be a liability for a China Expert? Not necessarily—at least not as long as he can hide it as well as his basic ignorance. The Expert should in all circumstances say nothing, but he should say it at great length, in four or five volumes, thoughtfully and from a prestigious vantage point. The Expert cultivates Objectivity, Balance, and Fair-Mindedness; in any conflict between your subjectivity and his subjectivity, these qualities enable him, at the crucial juncture, to lift himself by his bootstraps high up into the realm of objectivity, from whence he will arbitrate in all serenity and deliver the final conclusion. The Expert is not emotional; he always remembers that there are two sides to a coin. I think that even if you were to confront him with Auschwitz, for example, he would still be able to say that one should not have the arrogance to measure by one's own subjective standards Nazi values, which were, after all, quite *different*. After every statement, the Expert cautiously points to the theoretical possibility of also stating the opposite; however, when presenting opinions or facts that run counter to his own private prejudices, he will be careful not to lend them any real significance—though, at the same time, he will let them discreetly stand as emergency exits, should his own views eventually be proved wrong.

Ross Terrill, an Australian writer now settled in the United States, has been acclaimed there as the ultimate China Expert. I think he fully qualifies for the title.

Between the Charybdis of Professor Friedman and the Scylla of Madame Han Suyin, Mr. Terrill has been able to steer a skillful middle course. I would not go so far as to say that he has never imparted to his readers much useful insight on China (actually, I am afraid he has misled them rather seriously on several occasions); nevertheless, unlike his less subtle colleagues, he has managed to navigate safely through treacherous and turbulent waters and to keep his Expertise afloat against tremendous odds. By this sign you can recognize a genuine Expert: once an Expert, always an Expert.

When I was invited to review Terrill's biography of Mao,* I initially declined the suggestion; it seemed to me that the book in itself hardly warranted any comment—however, its significance lies more in what it omits than in what it commits. If I eventually accepted the task, it was not merely to offer a few observations on the "physiologie de l'Expert," but rather to take the opportunity to correct a bias of which I may have been guilty in the past when reviewing some of Terrill's earlier works. (These works include *800,000,000: The Real China* (1972), *Flowers on an Iron Tree* (1975), *The Future of China* (1978), and *The China Difference* (1979), which, like *China and Ourselves* (1970), is a collection of essays by various authors, edited and with an introduction by Terrill.)

My first encounter with his writings was inauspicious: opening at random his *Flowers on an Iron Tree*, I came upon a passage in which he described, as if he had visited it, a monument in China that had been razed to the ground years before. After that, it was hard for me to conjure away a vision of Terrill at work on his travelogue, busying himself with the study of outdated guidebooks without actually leaving his hotel room. For a long time this unfortunate *fausse note* was to color (unfairly, no doubt) the impression I had formed of Terrill's endeavors. Now, not only do I feel that my indignation was somewhat excessive, but I begin to see that in all the liberties Terrill takes with reality, there is always a principle and a method, both of which I completely overlooked at the time: when he sees things which are not there, at least he recognizes that these are things that *should be* there.

* *Mao: A Biography* (New York: Harper and Row, 1980).

This gives a kind of Platonic quality to his vision—it may be of little practical value, but it certainly testifies to the essential goodness and idealistic nature of his intentions.

All too often his statements are likely to provoke strong reactions in any informed reader; but these reactions, in their very violence, appear at once so totally out of tune with the style of this gentle and amiable man that one feels immediately ashamed of them. To attack Mr. Terrill seems as indecent as to kick a blind man's dog.

His basic approach is that of the perfect social hostess guiding the dinner-table conversation: be entertaining, but never controversial; avoid all topics that might disturb, give offense, or create unpleasantness; have something nice to say to everybody. (His *Mao*, for instance, is dedicated "To the flair for leadership which is craved in some countries today, and equally to the impulse of ordinary people to be free from the mystifications of leadership." His next work will probably be dedicated "To the Hare—and to the Hounds.")

Most of Terrill's utterances come across as bland and irresistible truisms. (For which he seems to share a taste with some famous statesmen. Remember de Gaulle: "China is a big country, inhabited by many Chinese"; or Nixon's comment on the Great Wall: "This is a great wall.") Here is a sampling from his books: "A billion people live in China, and we don't"; "Chopsticks are a badge of eternal China, yet it seems that eternal China might now be changing into another China"; "It is not very startling to say that China needs peace; so does every other country. But not every country gets peace"; "Change will not make China like the United States. But it will make post-Mao China different from Mao's China" (change generally does make things different from what they used to be, while different things are seldom similar); "Mao rules them, Nixon rules us, yet the systems of government have almost nothing in common"; "Could the Congo produce a

Mao? Could New Zealand?" (One is tempted to add: Could Luxembourg produce a Mao? Could Greenland? Or Papua New Guinea? The possibilities of variation on this theme are rich indeed.)

Under this relentless *tir de barrage* of tautologies the reader feels progressively benumbed. Sometimes, however, he is jerked out of his slumber by one of Terrill's original discoveries: "Superstitions are gone that used to make rural people of China see themselves as a mere stick or bird rather than an aware individual." If he genuinely believes that in pre-Communist China people saw themselves as "a stick or bird," we can more easily understand why he deems Maoist society to have achieved such a "prodigious social progress."

Terrill claimed that he was not a proponent of Maoism, but he made no secret of his admiration and sympathy for the regime ("[it is] somewhat absurd for non-Chinese to think of themselves as 'Maoists.' To be Maoist—when far from China—is hardly helpful to China, one's own society, or the relationship between the two. The editors of this book [*China and Ourselves*] are certainly not Maoists. They admire the Chinese revolution.")—this very regime which, as we now learn from the *People's Daily* and from Deng Xiaoping himself (and even, to some extent, from Terrill's latest writings!) went off the track as early as 1957, and ended up in a decade of near civil war and of "feudal-fascist terror."

Terrill visited China several times; his most extensive investigations, resulting in his influential *800,000,000: The Real China*, were conducted during the early 1970s—a time that was, by the reckoning of the Chinese themselves, one of the bleakest and darkest periods in their recent history. The country that had been bled white by the violence of the "Cultural Revolution" was frozen with fear, sunk into misery; it could hardly breathe under the cruel and cretinous tyranny of the Maoist Gang. Though it is only now that the Chinese press can describe that sinister era in full and harrowing detail, its horror was so pervasive that even foreigners, however insensitive and well insulated against the Chinese reality, could not fail to perceive it (though it is true, sadly, that too few of them dared at the time to say so publicly). Yet what did Terrill see? "To be frank, my weeks in China exceeded expectations. . . . The 1971 visit deepened my admiration for China and its people. . . ." In that hour of ferocious oppression, suffering, and despair, of humiliation and anguish, he enjoyed "the peace of the brightly colored hills and valleys of China . . . the excellence of Chinese cuisine. . . ."

Do not think, however, that his enjoyment was merely that of a tourist: "I happen, too, to be moved by the social gains of the Chinese revolution. In a magnificent way, it has healed the sick, fed the hungry and given security to the ordinary man of China." Maoism was "change with a purpose . . . the purposive change bespeaks strength, independence, leadership that was political power in the service of values." "China is a world which is sterner in its political imperatives but which in human terms may be a simpler and more relaxed world." How much more relaxed? Even though the country is tightly run, "this near total control is not by police terror. The techniques of Stalinist terror—armed police everywhere, mass killings, murder of political opponents, knocks on the door at three A.M., then a shot—are not evident in China today. . . . Control is more psychological than by physical coercion . . . the method of control is amazingly lighthanded by Communist standards. . . ." "The lack of a single execution by the state of a top Communist leader is striking . . . even imprisonment of a purgee is rare. . . . Far more common has been the milder fate of Liu Shaoqi and Deng Xiaoping in 1966. . . . They lived for many months in their own homes. No doubt they lounged in armchairs and read in the *People's Daily* the record of their misdeeds. . . . Liu was sent to a village, his health declined, and in 1973 he died of a cancer. . . ." (Actually, if one did not know of Terrill's essential decency, one might suspect him of making here a very sick joke indeed; Liu, who was very ill, was left by his tormentors lying in his own excrement, completely naked on the freezing concrete floor of his jail, till he died. As for Deng, though it is true that he was less roughly treated, he confessed in a recent interview that he spent all those years in constant fear of being assassinated.)

According to Terrill, Maoism has worked miracles in all areas: it "feeds a quarter of the world population and raises industrial output by ten percent per year"; it has achieved "thirty years of social progress"; thanks to it, even the blind can now see and the paralytic can walk, as Terrill himself observed when visiting a hospital: "The myth of Mao is functional to medicine and to much endeavor in China . . . it seemed to give [the patient] a mental picture of a world he could rejoin, and his doctors a vital extra ounce of resourcefulness. . . ." In conclusion, "there are things to be learned [from Maoism]: a public health system that serves all the people, a system of education that combines theory and practice, and economic growth that does not ravage the environment."

The impossibility of substantiating these fanciful claims never discouraged Terrill; for him, it was enough to conjure up those mythical achievements by a method of repetitive incantation, reminiscent of the Bellman's in Lewis Carroll:

Just the place for a Snark! I have said it twice:
That alone should encourage the crew.
Just the place for a Snark! I have said it thrice:
What I tell you three times is true.

Alas! After he had said it three times, there came the turn of the Chinese to talk, and they told the world quite a different story. Not only the dissenters writing on the Democracy Wall in Peking, but even the Communist leadership itself was to expose in gruesome detail the dark reality of Maoism: the bloody purges, the random arrests, tortures, and executions; the famines; the industrial mismanagement; the endemic problems of unemployment, hunger, delinquency; the stagnation and regression of living standards in the countryside; the corruption of the cadres; the ruin of the educational system; the paralysis and death of cultural life; the large-scale destruction of the natural environment; the sham of the agricultural models, of Maoist medicine.

As a result of these official disclosures, Terrill has now to a large extent already effected his own *aggiornamento: Mao*, his latest book, as well as some of his recent articles, reflects this new candor. Sometimes it does not square too well with the picture presented by his earlier writings—but who cares? Readers' amnesia will always remain the cornerstone of an Expert's authority.

The *People's Daily* has already apologized to its readers for "all the lies and distortions" it carried in the past, and has even warned its readers against "the false, boastful, and untrue reports" that it "still often carries." The China Experts used to echo it so faithfully—will they, this time again, follow suit and offer similar apologies to their own readers?

Or perhaps they were living in a state of pure and blessed ignorance. It is a fact that *official* admissions of Maoist bankruptcy are a very recent phenomenon; nevertheless, for more than twenty years, voices of popular dissent have been heard constantly in China, turning sometimes into thunderous outcry. These voices were largely ignored in Terrill's works; having first carefully stuffed his ears with Maoist cotton, he then wonders why he can hear so little, and concludes, "To be sure, it is very hard for us to measure the feelings of the Chinese people on any issue"!

Terrill's approach ignores the very existence of Maoist atrocities. Whenever this is not feasible, two tactics are simultaneously applied.

Tactic number one: similar things also happen in the so-called
democracies—"The Chinese had their own Watergate, and
worse." (Note the use of "worse"; compare with "Smith cut himself while shaving, Jones had his head cut off on the guillotine;
Jones's cut was worse.") Or again, "Red Guards smash the fingers of a pianist because he has been playing Beethoven's music.
To a Westerner who expects to be able to do his own thing, such
action suggests a tyranny without equal in history. In New York
City, two old folk die of cold because the gas company turned off
the heat in the face of an unpaid bill of twenty dollars. To a
Chinese who honors the elderly it seems callous beyond belief."
Terrill has curious ideas about the Chinese; his statement logically means that in China, smashing the fingers of a pianist is a
practice that provokes no revulsion because Chinese do not cultivate individual taste in music; moreover, he would have us believe that, for the Chinese, it is perfectly acceptable to smash a
pianist's fingers so long as the pianist is reasonably young. . . .
As regards the elderly New York couple, it would not be true to
say that their tragedy only met with indifference in the West: actually, it created a feeling of scandal to the point that it was reported in the press and hence could come to Mr. Terrill's
attention; I do not believe that the kind of thing that happened
to the elderly New York couple would attract much attention in
China. Not because the Chinese are particularly callous, but for
the simple reason that they have already used up all their tears,
mourning for *hundreds and thousands* of elderly people—cadres,
teachers, etc.—who died not as a result of neglect and administrative indifference, but because they were tortured to death by
Red Guards on the rampage. Moreover, if a moral equivalence
can be drawn between accidental death and willful murder, I

suppose that the next step for Terrill would be to write off political executions in totalitarian regimes by putting them on a par with traffic casualties in democracies.

The second tactic develops directly out of the notion according to which the smashing of pianists' fingers should be somewhat more acceptable in countries that have no individualistic tradition: we should endeavor "to perceive China on her own terms." Once more, the idea is not to hear what the Chinese have to say on the subject of Maoism—an initiative that Terrill never takes ("it is very hard for us to measure the feelings of the Chinese people on any issue"), but merely to see the People's Republic through orthodox official Maoist eyes. A logical extension of this principle would be to say that Nazi Germany should be perceived in a Hitlerian perspective, or that, to understand the Soviet system, one should adopt a Stalinist point of view (so sadly missing in, for example, the works of Solzhenitsyn or Nadezhda Mandelstam). Here we come to Terrill's fundamental philosophy: it is indeed (in the words of one of his titles), "the China difference."

Things happened in Maoist China that were ghastly by any standard of common decency. Even the Communist authorities in Peking admit this much today. Terrill maintains, however, that, China being "different," such standards should not apply. Look at the cult of Mao, for instance—it was grotesque and demeaning, and the hapless Chinese experienced it exactly as such. Not so, says Terrill, who knows better; being Chinese and thus different, they ought to have thoroughly enjoyed the whole exercise: "To see these pictures of Mao in China is to be less shocked than to see them on the printed page far from China. This is not our country or a country we can easily understand, but the country of Mao. . . . The cult of Mao is not *incredible* as it seems outside China. It becomes odd only when it encounters our world. . . . It is odd for us because we have no consciousness of Chinese social modes. . . ." (Meanwhile, Mr. Terrill has changed his mind on this question; in his latest book, he now qualifies the cult of Mao as "grotesque." Such a shift should not surprise—earlier on, he told us that we always "evaluate China from shifting grounds"; he recalls, for instance, that when he first visited China in 1964, he was still a churchgoer and, as such, felt critical of the fact that the Maoists closed churches; but a decade later, as he was no longer going to church, the closed churches did not bother him anymore: "I saw the issue under a fresh lens. I did not put the matter in the forefront of my view of China, and as a result, I saw a different China." One should pass this recipe to the *Chinese* churchgoers; it might help them to take a lighter view of their present condition.)

Following the fall of Madame Mao, the Chinese expressed eloquently the revulsion they felt for her "model operas" (and indeed, it seems that mere common sense should have enabled anyone to imagine how sophisticated audiences normally react to inferior plays); yet Terrill prefers to consider the issue from the angle of "the China difference" and thus produces this original comment: "When Mao's last wife rode high in the arts, there were only nine approved items performed on China's national stage. Such a straitjacket over the mental life of hundreds of millions of people seems amazing to a Westerner. Why did the theater-loving Chinese people put up with it? Again, we can glimpse the size of the gulf between the Chinese values and our own by considering one of their questions: How can a people with the traditions of the American Revolution tolerate the cruelty and inefficiency of having some seven percent unemployed?" I wonder if the thought of the seven percent unemployed in America ever helped frustrated theatergoers in China to put up with idiotic plays; I even doubt that this same thought ever helped the *millions* of unemployed Chinese to put up with their own condition, which is much worse than the Americans', since the Chinese state does not grant them any unemployment benefits.

Having analyzed at length Terrill's method and philosophy, I have very little to add concerning his latest effort. Up to the time of the "Cultural Revolution," the life of Mao had already been studied by a number of serious and competent scholars. In this area, Terrill does not shed new light; he produces rather an anecdotal adaptation of his predecessors' works, with plenty of dialogue, local color, and exotic scenery.

It is only on the subject of Mao's last years that Terrill might have provided an original contribution. Unfortunately, the diplomatic constraints that he imposed upon himself when dealing with topics that are still taboo for the Peking bureaucracy prevented him from tackling seriously the two central crises of Mao's twilight: on the one hand his attempts at destroying Zhou Enlai, and on the other the emergence of a popular anti-Mao movement that culminated in the historic Tian'anmen demonstration of April 5, 1976. On the first point, though he has already noticeably shifted his views, Terrill remains unable to confront the issue squarely—as this would entail the admission that the "Gang of Four," which persecuted Zhou until his death, was actually a "Gang of Five" led, inspired, and protected by Mao himself. On the second point, he entirely ignores the vast, spontaneous, and articulate movement of anti-Maoist dissent (the famous "Li Yizhe" Manifesto of 1974 is not even mentioned) and curtly dismisses its climax—the April Fifth Movement, whose importance in Chinese contemporary history already ranks on a par with the May Fourth Movement—terming it a mere "riot," a "melee" barely worth one page of sketchy and misleading description.

If these failures tend to disqualify *Mao* as historiography, the book still presents in its form and style a quaint charm that will certainly enchant readers of the old *Kai Lung Unrolls His Mat* series: chronological indications are mostly provided in terms of "Year of the Rat" or "Year of the Snake"; Terrill's disarming weakness for zoomorphic similes finds new outlets: since Mao once described his own character as half tiger and half monkey, we are kept informed, at every turn of his career, of what the tiger does, and what the monkey: "It irritated the monkey in him that Lin Biao spoke of absolute authority," and so forth. These touches will delight Terrill's younger readers, while adolescents may find more enjoyment in passages such as this description of Mao's accession to full power: "Jiangxi had been mere masturbation, alongside this full intercourse with the radiant bride of China."

AFTERWORD

My publisher has asked me to write an afterword to update this book. At first I was reluctant to comply with the request as I felt that it betrayed a certain misunderstanding of the nature and purpose of my essays. On second thought, however, I realized that some readers might well entertain similar misconceptions; hence, a short note of clarification would perhaps not be superfluous after all.

To those readers who are merely looking for the latest information on current socio-politico-economic developments in China, I would rather suggest that instead of purchasing this book they simply buy today's newspaper. There they will prob-

ably find most of what they want to know, at considerably less
expense. Yet the only drawback of today's newspaper is that tomorrow it will be out of date.

Arthur Koestler said: "If you were to ask me what a writer's
ambition in life should be, I would answer with a formula. A writer's ambition should be to trade a hundred contemporary readers
for ten readers in ten years, and for one reader in a hundred
years." (The trouble, of course, is that a hundred readers today
can significantly contribute to the wealth of a publisher, whereas
one reader in a hundred years is not likely to help him balance
his budget.)

When considering the timeliness and relevance of books (as
opposed to daily papers), it should also be noted that the question
to ask is not necessarily: How long can they remain topical? But
sometimes: How long will it take before they finally become topical? For instance, a perceptive critic recently suggested that
Custine's *Lettres de Russie* are far more accurate as a prophetic
intuition of the Soviet Union that we can see today than as a description of the Russian scene Custine observed 150 years ago.

The essays in this collection deal essentially with history, political ethics, ideas, and culture, and also with the problem of
how the West interprets China. Although, by their very nature,
such topics are not likely to be too much affected by the ups and
downs of everyday politics, all references to current affairs and
events made in these articles have been carefully updated to the
time of proofreading. Only one essay ventured directly into the
quicksands of straight political comment ("Is There Life After
Mao?"). In hindsight, it now seems to me that the disintegration
of the system I described has perhaps been developing faster
than I would have thought, and I may have underestimated the
depth of the political and social repercussions of the new economic reforms. Finally, the central question (which I am naturally unable to answer) is: To what extent does the historical

experience of the Soviet Union still constitute a valid projection of the future of China? Or, on the contrary, to what extent did Mao's "Cultural Revolution" succeed in injecting a completely new and irreducible component into the chemistry of the regime, which in turn might lead to its eventual destruction and meta- morphosis?

As I have already observed, China-watching (which is not my trade) is the safest of all occupations: whatever you may predict is bound to become true one day or another—all you need is a little patience. Thus, those who declare that, in the end, nothing ever changes in China are probably not wrong, and those who put their faith in China's infinite capacity for organic transfor- mation and adaptation are certainly right. It is not by chance that the poets, painters, and mystics of ancient China appear to have been constantly fascinated by the paradox of the waterfall, whose perpetual motion suggests perfect immobility. Hasn't change al- ways been at the heart of China's unique continuity?

June 1985

Appendixes

SOME SAYINGS
OF LU XUN*

■   ■   ■   ■   ■

LITERATURE

It seems to me that the spoken and written word are signs of failure. Whoever is truly measuring himself against fate has no time
for such things. As to those who are strong and winning, most of
the time they keep silent. Consider, for instance, the eagle when
it swoops upon a rabbit: it is the rabbit that squeals, not the eagle. Similarly, when a cat catches a mouse, the mouse squeaks,
but not the cat. Or again, remember the Tyrant of Chu: in his

* Translated from the Chinese by Simon Leys.

golden days, as he was leading his victorious armies from one end of the country to the other, he did not say much. When he began to play the poet and to sing lyric laments, his troops were beaten and he knew that his own end was near.

When a man feels the pangs of loneliness, he is able to create. As soon as he reaches detachment, he ceases to create, for he loves no more.

Every creation originates in love.

Creation, even when it is a mere outpouring from the heart, wishes to find a public. By definition, creation is sociable. Yet it can be satisfied with merely one single reader: an old friend, a lover.

PSYCHOLOGY

When you talk with a Famous Thinker, you should pretend now and then that you do not understand him fully. If you did not understand him at all, he would despise you; and if you were to understand him too well, he would resent it—whereas, if now and then you do not understand him fully, this will suit him fine.

Women have a mother-nature and a daughter-nature; there are no women with a wife-nature. The quality of wife is an acquired character; it is a combination of mother and daughter.

Whoever thinks he is objective must already be half drunk.

Trust only him who doubts.

On the ground floor, a sick man is dying. A gramophone is blaring next door. In the hallway, children are playing. Upstairs, two men are laughing loudly. There is the din of a mah-jongg game. In the middle of the river, on a boat, a woman cries because her mother just died.

People do not communicate their happiness or their grief; I find that they are merely being noisy.

A man who wishes to commit suicide may sometimes waver in front of a vast ocean, or hesitate as he imagines his own body rotting under a fierce sun. Yet, should he happen to come across a clear pool in a cool autumn night, he will jump.

As I hate a certain number of people, it is quite natural that a certain number of people hate me. In this way, at least, I feel that I am fully alive. Conversely, if I were to encounter kind compliments everywhere, I would feel utterly insulted.

GREAT MEN

Schopenhauer made this observation: when estimating the size of a man, one must follow opposite methods if one wishes to know his spiritual stature or his physical height. The latter decreases with distance, whereas the former increases.

As a great man appears smaller when seen at close quarters, where his blemishes and warts are more conspicuous, he also becomes more like us: he is no longer a god, or a miraculous creature, or a supernatural being, he is simply a man. But this is precisely where his greatness lies.

Our forefathers, however dumb, managed after a few thousand years of reflection to elaborate a subtle recipe to control people: crush all those whom you can crush; as for others, put them on a pedestal. By putting them on a pedestal, you can also control them—you merely need to whisper constantly in their ears, "Do as I tell you, otherwise I shall bring you down."

When the Chinese suspect someone of being a potential troublemaker, they always resort to two methods: they crush him, or they hoist him on a pedestal.

Young people who wish to forge ahead generally dream of finding a guide for themselves. Personally, I dare to affirm that they will not find any, and it is all the better for them. No clearsighted man would ever agree to be taken for a guide; as for those who do not decline to be put in such a role, are they really qualified to lead the way? People who boast that they know the way are invariably gentlemen of mature age, respectably dull and pedantic, mellow and smooth. However, if they think that they know the way, they are cheating themselves. If they really knew it, they would have reached their goal long ago, and they would be too busy with real issues to still find the time to play at being guides. It is like the monks who preach about Buddha's paradise, or the Taoists who sell "immortality pills"; all these peddlers-of-eternal-life end up in the same cemetery—they make me laugh.

Young people, what need have you to follow the trendy slogans of these intellectual leaders? You ought better to gather some comrades and pool together all your energies; go forward in one common impetus, following what appears to be the path of survival. All together, you will never be short of strength. If you encounter a deep forest, you can always hack your way through; you can open up the wilderness, you can dig wells in the desert. Why should you stick to the old ruts, and beg for the guidance of these wretched guides?

CHINA

John Stuart Mill said that tyranny makes people cynical. He didn't realize that there would be republics to make them silent.

Generally speaking, Chinese hate Buddhist monks and nuns; they hate Moslems, and they hate Christians. But they do not hate Taoist priests.

Whoever understands the reason for this has understood half of China.

Of course, whether we are massacred by our own people, or we are massacred by foreigners, does not amount exactly to the same thing. Thus, for instance, if a man slaps his own face, he will not feel insulted, whereas if someone else slaps him, he will feel angry. However, when a man is so cretinous that he can slap his own face, he fully deserves to be slapped by any passerby.

We let ourselves be turned all too easily into slaves. And the worst is that once we have become slaves, we derive much satisfaction from it.

Before the revolution we were slaves. And now we are slaves of former slaves.

Lies written in ink cannot obscure a truth written in blood.

Once upon a time, there was a country whose rulers completely succeeded in crushing the people; and yet they still believed that the people were their most dangerous enemy. The rulers issued huge collections of statutes, but none of these volumes could actually be used, because in order to interpret them, one had to refer to a set of instructions that had never been made public. These instructions contained many original definitions. Thus, for instance, "liberation" meant in fact "capital execution"; "government official" meant "relative, friend, or servant of an influential politician," and so on. The rulers also issued codes of laws that were marvelously modern, complex, and complete; however, at the beginning of the first volume, there was one blank page; this blank page could be deciphered only by those who knew the instructions—which did not exist. The first three articles on this invisible page were as follows: "Article 1: Some cases must be treated with special leniency. Article 2: Some cases must be treated with special severity. Article 3: This does not apply in all cases." Naturally, there were also courts of justice; however, the accused, who were aware of the invisible articles, knew better than to defend themselves in front of their judges, since they knew that only a hardened criminal would claim to be innocent, and that an accused who has the cheek to plead not guilty deserves to be treated with "special severity." Of course, there were also appeals courts and a Supreme Court; but whoever was aware of the invisible articles knew better than to appeal against a judgment, since only a hardened criminal would appeal against his sentence, thus deserving to be treated with "special severity."

When clever fellows begin to praise someone—be he a wealthy old man, an actress, or their boss—it is naturally in the hope to derive some benefit from this activity. Yet, for the ordinary people, the main purpose of all sycophancy is simply to ward off catastrophes. Consider, for instance, the various gods that are being worshipped in China—nine times out of ten, they are malefic powers. No need to mention the God of Fire and the God of Plague—even the God of Wealth is seen in the shape of a horrible monster, half snake and half hedgehog. Simply speaking, in China, whoever is the object of a cult must be a very dubious character.

I said that for China the first imperative was "survival," but I must immediately add that by "survival" I do not merely mean to eke a living by disgraceful means. . . . In this sense, there is a formula that it seems no one has thought of yet—and it is the model offered by Number One Prison in Peking. The inmates need not worry anymore that the neighbors' house may be on fire; their two daily meals are guaranteed; cold and hunger cannot affect them; their shelter is stable and soundly built, and there is no danger that the roof will cave in. As they are carefully watched by their jailer, they have no opportunities for new brushes with the law. They are being afforded superb protection against burglars. One could not dream of a safer place. Only one thing is missing—freedom.

POLITICS

If there are still men who really want to live in this world, they should first dare to speak out, to laugh, to cry, to be angry, to accuse, to fight—that they may at least cleanse this accursed place of its accursed atmosphere!

You tell me, "Sheep will always be sheep. What else can they do but obediently walk in line to the slaughterhouse? As to the pigs, which have to be dragged, which jump, squeal, and try to run away, in the end they still cannot escape their fate. Why such desperate efforts? Is it not a sheer waste of energy?"

But this is to say that even when faced with death, one should behave like a sheep; thus the world will be in peace, and everyone will be spared much trouble.

Very well, this is perhaps an excellent solution. However, have you ever considered wild boars? With their tusks they can force even experienced hunters to keep at a distance. Actually, all that an ordinary pig needs to do is to run away from the sty where the swineherd was keeping it locked, and reach the forest—and in no time it will grow such tusks.

Whoever was in power wishes for a restoration. Whoever is now in power is in favor of the status quo. Whoever is not yet in power demands reforms. The situation is generally such. Generally!

Revolution, counterrevolution, nonrevolution.

Revolutionaries are massacred by counterrevolutionaries. Counterrevolutionaries are massacred by revolutionaries. Nonrevolutionaries are sometimes taken for revolutionaries, and then they are massacred by counterrevolutionaries, or again they are taken for counterrevolutionaries, and then they are massacred by revolutionaries. Sometimes, also, they are not taken for anything in particular, but they are still massacred by revolutionaries and by counterrevolutionaries.

Revolution. To revolutionize revolution; to revolutionize the revolution of revolution; to rev . . .

I naturally believe that there will be a future, but I do not waste my time imagining its radiant beauty.

Rather than discussing how to reach the future, it seems to me that we ought to think first about the present. Even if the present is desperately dark, I do not wish to leave it.

Will tomorrow be free from darkness? We'll talk about that tomorrow. Meanwhile, let us busy ourselves with transforming *today*.

HOPE

Hope can be neither affirmed nor denied. Hope is like a path in the countryside: originally there was no path—yet, as people are walking all the time in the same spot, a way appears.

THE FIFTH MODERNIZATION: DEMOCRACY*

By Wei Jingsheng

■ Wei Jingsheng belongs to the generation of "Mao's children." He was born with the People's Republic, the son of Party cadres. During the "Cultural Revolution" he became a Red Guard leader. For him, as for many of his companions, this experience afforded a dramatic revelation of the real nature of Maoist politics.

Shortly after his return to power, Deng Xiaoping found it expedient to allow a brief "thaw." Brave and idealistic young people took advantage of this short-lived "liberalization" to demand that the Maoist totalitarian heritage be repudiated and that democracy be established. Wei's manifesto was one of the most articulate expressions of the "Democratic Movement." It elicited at once such wide popular support that the Communist authorities decided to suppress the movement and to arrest all its leaders. On October 16, 1979, at the end of a shameless parody of a trial, and on the basis of trumped-up charges, a Peking court sentenced Wei Jingsheng to fifteen years in prison.

■　　　　■　　　　■　　　　■　　　　■

* Translated from the Chinese by Simon Leys.

I f newspapers and the radio have now stopped bashing our ears with their deafening propaganda catchwords on the theme of "class struggle," it is partly because this was the magic abracadabra of the "Gang of Four." But mostly because the masses were fed up with it; you cannot make people march anymore to that tune.

There is a law of history according to which as long as the old does not disappear, the new cannot come into existence. Now that the old is gone for good, everyone is scanning the horizon in the hope of seeing the emergence of the new. As the saying goes: "God would never disappoint the faithful." Hence, a fantastic new formula was invented and is being served to us now. They call it "The Four Modernizations." Chairman Hua (our "wise leader") and Vice-Chairman Deng (who, in the eyes of some people, is even wiser and greater) managed to defeat the "Gang of Four," thus making it possible again to dream of democracy and prosperity—a dream for which heroic people shed their blood in Tian'anmen Square, on April 5, 1976.

After the arrest of the "Gang of Four," the people ardently hoped for the return of Deng; and in their delusion that he would "restore capitalism," they turned him into the living symbol of their movement. Eventually, Deng was reinstalled in the central leadership of the State and of the Party; and this event was greeted by the entire nation with indescribable enthusiasm and emotion.

After that, alas! our odious political system was not amended in the slightest. As for the freedom and democracy that the people expected, even the very words cannot be mentioned. The living conditions of the population have not changed; "salary increases" were largely canceled by the astronomical rising of prices. As for "capitalist restoration," it seems that the system of production bonuses is going to be reintroduced—precisely what the Fathers of Marxism-Leninism used to stigmatize as "the

invisible whip under which workers suffer maximum exploitation." It is now announced that the methodical policy of "cretin-
ization of the masses" has been abandoned. Though the people
are not to be kept anymore under the authority of a "Great Helmsman," they are now under the direction of a "Wise Leader" who
will see to it that they "catch up with and overtake the most advanced countries of the world," such as England, the United
States, Japan, and . . . Yugoslavia! To "make revolution" is not
fashionable nowadays. Now, if you wish to achieve a brilliant career, the best way is again to work for a university degree. The
people need no longer suffer the wearisome drivel of "class struggle." Now it is the "Four Modernizations" that have become the
new panacea. Needless to say, we still must obey the orders of
the central authorities. Follow the guide dutifully, and all your
beautiful dreams will materialize. . . .

There is an old Chinese saying that tells of "feeding the people
by painting cakes," and there is another one of "quenching thirst
by contemplating plums." The satirical spirit of this old wisdom
truly reflects long political experience. If history is actually a
constant progression, how could one still hope today to swindle
the public with those same crude stratagems that had already
been exposed long ago by our ancestors? And yet there are still
people who believe they can cheat the world with such tricks,
and who actually proceed in this fashion.

Thus, during these last few decades, the Chinese people doc-
ilely followed a "Great Helmsman" who fed them with cakes that
he painted by using a brush called "communism," and who
quenched their thirst by dangling in front of their noses plums
that were called "Great Leap Forward" or "Three Red Flags."
And the people kept on bravely marching forward, tightening
their belts. . . . After having suffered this regime with considerable fortitude for thirty years, the people eventually understood: like the monkey who attempts to grasp the moon, they were

condemned to remain forever empty-handed. That is why, as soon as Vice-Chairman Deng launched his new program, "Back to Reality," the masses supported him with enthusiasm, showing their approval with a voice as formidable as the roaring of the ocean. Everyone expected that Deng, applying his famous principle "to reach truth from facts," would submit the recent past to critical investigation, and that he would lead the people toward a worthy future.

And yet, what is actually happening now? Some gentlemen come to warn us earnestly: "Marxism-Leninism and Mao Zedong Thought remain the foundation of all there is on earth; no valid utterance can be formulated without referring to it." Or again: "Chairman Mao is the savior of the people," and "Without the Communist Party, there would be no New China"—which amounts to saying, "Without Chairman Mao, there would be no New China." Now, if anyone questions these affirmations, there are good medicines to cure him of his skepticism! Some others lecture us: "The Chinese people need to be led by a strong man. If the modern despot is even tougher than his feudal predecessors, this merely shows his greatness. The Chinese people have no need for democracy, except when it comes properly 'centralized'; in any other form, it is not worth a penny. You have little faith? As you wish. For your kind of people, there is always room in our jails. . . ."

Nevertheless, they still leave you one open path. *Forward march!* Within the framework of the "Four Modernizations," close all ranks, and cut out the nonsense, all you dutiful pack-horses of the Revolution! At the end of the road you will reach Paradise—the utopia of Communism—with the "Four Modernizations." Furthermore, well-meaning persons still come forward to lavish their wisdom on us: "If these perspectives still fail to stir your enthusiasm, apply yourselves seriously to the study of Marxism-Leninism and Mao Zedong Thought! Your lack of enthusiasm results from your deficient theoretical understanding, and the very fact that you do not understand the theory precisely proves its sublime depth. Come on, be good fellows now—anyway, the authorities that be, ordained by history, will not allow you any alternative. . . ."

I beg you all—do not let these political swindlers cheat you yet again! Rather than swallow what we know to be a dupery, why not, for once, simply rely on our own resources? The cruel experiences of the Cultural Revolution have opened our eyes. Let us try to discover by ourselves what is to be done.

WHY IS DEMOCRACY NECESSARY?

This question has been discussed at length now for many centuries. More recently, the various people who put forward their views on the Democracy Wall explained thoroughly why democracy is infinitely better than despotism.

"The people are the masters of history"—is this true, or is it an empty phrase? It is both true *and* an empty phrase. We say that it is true because without the people's strength, without the people's participation, no history is conceivable (with or without "the Great Helmsman" and other "Wise Leaders"). From this point of view, it is obvious that without a new Chinese people there could be no "New China"; and it is not thanks to Chairman Mao that this "New China" came into existence. Vice-Chairman Deng thanked Chairman Mao for having saved his life—we can understand and forgive his reaction—however, should he not rather thank the *people*, who, with their outcry, succeeded in returning him to office? How does he dare to say now to the people: "You should not criticize Chairman Mao—after all, he saved my life!" From such an episode, it appears clear that a saying such as "the people are the masters of history" is mere hollow chatter. Its emptiness is plain, because we see that, in fact, the people are deprived of any possibility of determining their fate according to the wishes of the majority. All the achievements of the people are always credited to someone else, all the rights of the people are confiscated to weave a garland for someone else. In these conditions, can we still say that the people are the masters? They look rather like docile slaves. Even though the people remain theoretically creators and masters of history, in actual fact their role is merely to provide legions of respectful and silent servants, and to serve as clay in the hands of the real masters.

The people need democracy. When they demand democracy, they simply demand that which originally belonged to them. Whoever dares to deny them democracy is nothing but a shameless bandit, even more despicable than the capitalist who robs the workers' sweat and blood.

Do the people now enjoy democracy? No. Is it that the people do not want to be their own masters? Of course they do! It is precisely for this reason that the Communist Party defeated the Kuomintang. After its victory, what came out of all the earlier promises? First they changed the slogan of "People's Democratic Dictatorship" into "Dictatorship of the Proletariat." And then the last democratic leftovers, which a tiny handful of people were still enjoying at the top, disappeared too, to be replaced by the personal despotism of "the Great Leader." Thus, on "the Great Leader's" orders, Peng Dehuai was dismissed and dragged in the mud, for having dared to vent some grumbles at an internal gathering of Party leaders. So it was that a new formula appeared: "Since the Leader is so great, a blind faith in his person could only bring increasing happiness to the people." At the time, the people accepted this formula, partly because they were forced to do so and partly because they were willing. But what is the situation now? Are the people really happier, more prosperous?

The inescapable truth is that today the people are more miserable, unhappy, and backward than before. How could such a situation develop? This is the first question we should examine. What should we do? This is the second question we must study.

Today it is perfectly irrelevant to try to determine the balance account of Mao Zedong's achievements and mistakes. Originally it was he himself who suggested such an assessment; for him, this was a defensive maneuver. The question that the people should now be asking is this: Without Mao Zedong's personal despotism, could China ever have fallen as low as we see her today? Or are we to believe that Chinese people are stupid or lazy or devoid of any desire to improve their lot? We know very well that this is not the case. Then what happened? The answer is obvious: the Chinese have taken a path they should never have entered; if they followed it, it is because a despot, who knew how to peddle his trash shrewdly, simply took them for a ride. On the other hand, he did not leave them very much choice: "You disagree? then you will be given a personal dose of dictatorship!" Moreover, the people were kept in complete ignorance of all alternatives, and were persuaded that this was the sole feasible way. What a swindle! Is there still any point in calculating exactly how many kudos should be awarded to its perpetrator?

What is this way called? I am told it is called "the socialist way." According to the Marxist theoreticians, under socialism the masses—also known as the "proletariat"—hold all political power. Go and ask Chinese workers: "Apart from the wretched salary that you are given every month, just to prevent you from starving, what rights do you have? What power do you have? Whose masters are you? Alas, you can control nothing—not even your own marriage!"

Socialism is supposed to guarantee to every producer the right to enjoy the fruits of his own labor after he has discharged his duties toward society. And yet, for you, is there any limit to the burden of your duties? What is allocated to you is precisely this wretched salary, "barely enough to sustain the energy necessary to meet production requirements"! Socialism is supposed to ensure that every citizen has the right to be educated, to develop his individual talents, and many other rights—but we see no trace of all this in our lives. The only thing we can see is "the dictatorship of the proletariat" and this new variation of the "Russian-style despotism," which is now "Chinese-style despotism." Who can really believe that this socialist way contains any recipe for the happiness of the people?

Is this the kind of socialism that Marx envisioned and that the people are hoping for? Obviously not. What is it, then? We would laugh if it were not so sad—it resembles precisely the kind of "social feudalism" described in the *Manifesto*, a kind of feudal monarchy in socialist garb. As we are instructed, the Soviet Union has already passed this stage of "social feudalism" and has now reached the superior stage of "social imperialism." Will the Chinese also have to follow the same historical itinerary?

There are some who believe that these negative aspects should be ascribed to the "social-fascist" tyranny of our social feudalism. I fully agree. There should, therefore, no longer be any question of assessing relative merits and shortcomings. Let me explain. German fascism, of stinking memory, was actually called National Socialism. It too was led by a tyrant; it too told the people to tighten their belts; it too deceived the people, assuring them, "You are a great nation!" Above all, it too suppressed basic democracy, because it saw clearly that democracy was the greatest danger for it, the most frightful enemy. Stalin and Hitler could shake hands and sign the famous German-Soviet pact, and on this basis the German and Russian peoples were condemned to suffer slavery and misery. Do we, too, need to continue suffering such slavery and misery? If we wish to break away from it, there is only one way—democracy. In other words, if we want to modernize our economy and science and defense and the like, we must first modernize our people. We must first modernize our social system.

THE FIFTH MODERNIZATION—WHICH DEMOCRACY?

Let me ask you one question: Why do we want modernization? Some people may feel that the way of life at the time of *The Dream of the Red Chamber* was already quite pleasant—just think of it: reading novels, dabbling in poetry, playing with charming girls, finding satisfaction of all needs without effort. . . . To bring this ideal up to date, one would just need to add the possibility of watching foreign films. Is that not paradise? You may say so. But the people should have their share of it. The people must be able to pursue real happiness, to enjoy advantages at least equal to those that are afforded to foreigners. All the people should be able to enjoy a prosperity equally distributed among the entire population. To reach such prosperity, the level of the productive forces in our society must first be raised. All of this is obvious enough, but one important question is often forgotten: Once the productive forces have increased, will the people be able to enjoy a more prosperous life? What we encounter here is the problem of distribution and exploitation.

After Liberation, during the first few decades, the Chinese people worked very hard, tightening their belts. They created considerable wealth. Where did all this wealth go? According to some, it was used to fatten various minidespotisms, such as Vietnam, for instance. Others say that it was used to fatten such people as Lin Biao, Jiang Qing, and other members of the "new capitalist class." Both of these views are correct. One thing is certain—the working classes never saw a single penny of it. This wealth was partly squandered by our "political swindlers," and partly given away to their Vietnamese and Albanian colleagues and crooks. Before his death, Mao Zedong was bothered by his old woman, who merely wanted to enjoy a few more thousand yuan from the budget. Yet, earlier on, he himself lightly squandered billions accumulated by the sweat and blood of the people, without giving it a thought—and this was at the time when a nation of beggars was hard-pressed to build socialism on empty bellies.

Today some people still come to praise Mao Zedong on the Democracy Wall; if they had eyes to see, how could they manage never to notice these things? Did they decide to remain blind? If they have still seen nothing, instead of wasting their time writing posters, they ought rather to go to the Peking railway station or around Yongding Gate, or simply take a stroll in the streets. Ask the visitors who come from the provinces: is it true that there are no more beggars? Do you believe that our beggars agree with giving our rice away to "Third World friends"—rice that, for them, is more precious than their own blood? Who cares to ask their opinion? The tragedy is that, in our so-called People's Republic, only those with their bellies full, enjoying wealth, leisure, and privileged lives, have the actual power to distribute wealth. Would it not be absolutely right for the people to take back this power from the hands of those gentlemen?

What is democracy? Genuine democracy means giving all powers to the workers' collective. Are workers unable to administer state powers? Yugoslavia has taken up this path and has proved that the people have no need for despots, large or small, and that they can, by themselves, look much better after their own interests.

What is genuine democracy? It is a system that allows the people to choose, at their own will, representatives who administer in the name of the people, in conformity with the people's will and interests. The people must retain the right to dismiss and replace their representatives at any time, to prevent them from abusing their powers and turning into oppressors. Is such a system actually feasible? In Europe and the United States, the people enjoy precisely this type of democracy. At will, they were able to dismiss their Nixon or de Gaulle or Tanaka, and if they so wish they can as well call them back, without any force interfering with the free exercise of their democratic prerogative. But, in our country, if in a private conversation you merely express the slightest doubt concerning the historical sublimity of our "Great Helmsman," Mao Zedong (even though he has already passed away), you immediately see in front of you the gaping gates of a jail where various special treatments, all quite beyond imagination, are awaiting you. If one compares the "democratic centralism" of the socialist countries with the democracy of the "exploiting classes" in capitalist regimes, one sees a difference as great as between night and day!

Is it true to say that if democratic rights were granted to the people, there would be a danger of falling into disorder and anarchy? On the contrary. Newspapers in our country recently exposed all the scandalous abuses that our despots, large and small, could perpetrate precisely because we have no democracy—*that* is the real disorder, the *real* anarchy! The problem of how to maintain democratic order is a problem of internal politics with which the people alone are competent to deal, and there is no need to call upon some feudal gentlemen, equipped with special powers, to take care of this problem for the people (for the purpose of these gentlemen is not to protect democracy, but to find a pretext to divest the people of their rights). Of course, these problems of internal politics are not simple, and to solve them will require a lengthy process during which mistakes will inevitably be committed, needing constant rectification.

But this is *our* business, and such a system is still a thousand times better than the arrogant tyranny of our present feudal aristocracy, providing no recourse against constant injustice. As for the people who worry at the idea that the establishment of democracy might produce chaos, they remind me of those who, just after the 1911 Republican Revolution, believed that a China without emperors would sink into chaos. Their conclusion is, "Let us patiently suffer oppression. . . ." Are they afraid that without a tyrant riding on their back, they might stumble and fall?

To those who entertain such worries, let me merely say this, very respectfully: We want to become the masters of our own destiny. We need no gods and no emperors; we believe in no savior; we want to direct our own lives. We do not want to be mere tools in the hands of despots with expansionist ambitions, who wish to use us to carry out a modernization geared to their own advantage. What we want is a modernization of the people's living conditions. The only reason we want to achieve modernization is to ensure democracy, freedom, and happiness for the people. Without this "fifth modernization" all other "modernizations" are nothing but lies.

Comrades, I launch this appeal to you: Let us all unite under the flag of democracy! Do not let us be cheated again by those slogans of "unity in stability" of which our despots are so fond. Totalitarian fascism can bring us only disaster. Entertain no more illusions concerning these people. Democracy is our only hope. If we give up our democratic rights, it is as if we fasten onto ourselves our own chains. Trust your own forces! We alone create human history! As for those who award themselves the titles of "Great Leaders" and "Great Teachers," and who have swindled the people of their most precious rights for several decades now, may they all go to hell!

I firmly believe that if production is put under control of the people, it will certainly increase, because the producers will work in their own interest. Life will become beautiful and good, because everything will be geared toward the improvement of the workers' living conditions. Society will be more just, because all rights and powers will be democratically wielded by all the workers.

I have no illusions—this ideal will not be reached without strenuous efforts; and in order to achieve it, the people must not count on the intervention of some providential hero. Yet I know that the Chinese people will not be discouraged by the many difficulties they will encounter on the way. The main thing is that the people must acquire a clear vision of the goal and an accurate assessment of the obstacles, and must, without hesitation, be able to crush the pathetic insects that try to hinder their progression.

FORWARD TOWARD MODERNIZATION:
ESTABLISHING DEMOCRACY

If the Chinese people wish to modernize, they must first establish democracy, they must first modernize China's social system. Democracy is not what Lenin says, a mere consequence of a certain stage of development of society. It is not merely the necessary product of a certain degree of development of the productive forces and the production relations. It is also the condition on which depends the very survival of the productive forces (and the production relations in this phase of development, or in a situation of superior development). Without democracy, society would sink into a stage of stagnation, and economic growth would encounter insuperable obstacles. Thus, as is shown by historical precedents, a democratic social system was always the prerequisite for any real development. Without this preliminary condition, it would not only be impossible to achieve any progress, but it would even be difficult merely to preserve the achievements obtained at a given level of development. The best evidence is provided by the situation to which our great country has been reduced after these last thirty years.

Why is human history oriented toward progress—which may also be called "modernization"? It is because mankind needs all the advantages that only a developed society can provide; it is because the social consequences of these advantages are the surest way to achieve the primordial objectives in its pursuit of happiness—which are freedom and democracy. The struggle of modern times is a struggle to achieve the maximum degree of freedom and democracy that mankind can contemplate.

Why, all through modern history, have reactionaries always united against democracy? Because democracy forms the main strength of their rivals—the masses of the people—and to them, the oppressors, it leaves no opportunity to bully the citizenry. The worst reactionaries hate nothing more than democracy; the truth of this has been clearly illustrated by the examples of Nazi Germany, the Soviet Union, and "the New China." Those who oppose democracy are the worst enemies of a society's peace and prosperity. This again has been clearly demonstrated in the history of Germany, the Soviet Union, and "the New China." People seek to be happy, societies try to develop; the struggle that they wage to achieve these objectives is essentially a struggle against the enemies of democracy, against fascist despots. This is clearly shown in the contemporary history of Germany, of the Soviet Union, and of China. In this struggle the victory of democracy over dictatorship automatically creates better conditions of development for society and allows this development to progress with greater speed. The history of the United States is the best example of this phenomenon.

Any struggle waged by the people to ensure happiness, peace, and prosperity must necessarily begin with a struggle to obtain democratic rights. Similarly, for a people to resist oppression and exploitation, the most essential objective must be the establishing of democracy. Let us bring all our strength into this battle for the establishment of democracy! The people's will is democratic; despotism, dictatorship, and totalitarianism are its most direct and most dangerous enemies.

Will these enemies let us establish democracy? Of course not. They will try by all means to hinder the progression of democracy. One of their most efficient methods is to cheat and deceive the people—all fascist despots keep repeating, "You enjoy the very best conditions in the whole world!"

Will democracy emerge by itself at the end of a natural and necessary evolution? Certainly not. On the way toward democracy, the smallest victory will exact a terrible price; let us have no illusions; democracy will be reached only after bloody sacrifices. The enemies of democracy try always to deceive the people, telling them: "The emergence and the disappearance of democracy are phenomena that result from an inner necessity; there is thus no need to spend any effort to bring it into existence. . . ."

Look rather at the teachings of history, true history, not the history written by Party hacks: genuine democracy, the only valid democracy, is nourished with the blood of martyrs and with the blood of tyrants. Every step forward toward democracy must overcome the frantic counterattacks launched by reactionary forces. The fact that democracy succeeds in defeating all these obstacles shows how dear it is to the people; it is the embodiment of all their hopes, which endows it with the irresistible impetus of a tidal wave. The Chinese people fear nothing; once they have clearly recognized which orientation they must follow, they will be able to overthrow their tyrants.

Can the struggle for democracy mobilize the Chinese people?

During the Cultural Revolution, for the first time they became aware of their own strength when they saw all the reactionary powers shaking with fear. But at that time the people still did not have a clear idea of the way they should proceed, and thus the democratic trend could not predominate. Hence it was all too easy for the tyrant to dominate, manipulate, and divert most of these struggles; he neutralized the movement by using in turn provocations, seductions, lies, and violent repression. Since the people, at that time, still had a religious respect for despots, they became the powerless toys and victims of the ruling tyrant as well as of all the other tyrants to come.

Twelve years later, however, the people have now identified their goal, they see clearly the way they should follow, they finally acknowledge their true banner—the flag of democracy.

The Democracy Wall in Xidan became their first fortress in the struggle against all reactionary forces. In this struggle, we shall overcome. As the propaganda phrase used to say: "The people will certainly liberate themselves"; but this time that wornout slogan is being given a new meaning. Blood will be shed, there will be new martyrs, persecution will become even more sinister; but the reactionary forces will never again succeed in obliterating our democratic flag in their poisonous mist. Let us all unite under this flag, which is great and true; let us march forward to secure peace and happiness for the people, to win our rights and our freedom, and to make our society truly modern!

(Posted on the Democracy Wall in Peking, December 5, 1978)

INDEX

241